First World War
and Army of Occupation
War Diary
France, Belgium and Germany

49 DIVISION
146 Infantry Brigade
Prince of Wales's Own (West Yorkshire Regiment)
1/7th Battalion
16 April 1915 - 31 May 1919

WO95/2795/1

The Naval & Military Press Ltd
www.nmarchive.com
Published in association with The National Archives

Published by

The Naval & Military Press Ltd

Unit 10 Ridgewood Industrial Park,

Uckfield, East Sussex,

TN22 5QE England

Tel: +44 (0) 1825 749494

www.naval-military-press.com

www.nmarchive.com

This diary has been reprinted in facsimile from the original. Any imperfections are inevitably reproduced and the quality may fall short of modern type and cartographic standards.

© **Crown Copyright**
Images reproduced by permission of The National Archives, London, England, 2015.

Contents

Document type	Place/Title	Date From	Date To
Heading	WO95/2795/1 1/7 Battalion West Yorkshire Regiment.		
Heading	49th Division 146th Infy Bde 1-7th Bn West Yorks Regt. Apr 1915-May 1919		
Heading	146th Inf. Bde. 49th Div. Battn. disembarked Boulogne from England 16.4.15. 1/7 Battn. The West Yorkshire Regiment. April (16/30.4.15) 1915-May 19		
War Diary	Boulogne	16/04/1915	16/04/1915
War Diary	Merville	17/04/1915	22/04/1915
War Diary	N of La Gorgue	23/04/1915	30/04/1915
Heading	146th Inf. Bde. 49th Div. 1/7th Battn. The West Yorkshire Regiment. May 1915		
War Diary	N of La Gorgue	01/05/1915	01/05/1915
War Diary	Bac St Maur	02/05/1915	05/05/1915
War Diary	In Trenches "D" Lines	06/05/1915	18/05/1915
War Diary	Rue Du Quisne	19/05/1915	21/05/1915
War Diary	In Trenches Q2, R2, S2	22/05/1915	29/05/1915
War Diary	Rue Du Quesne	30/05/1915	31/05/1915
Heading	146th Inf. Bde 49th Div. 1/7th Battn. The West Yorkshire Regiment June 1915		
War Diary	Rue Du Quesne	01/06/1915	04/06/1915
War Diary	In Trenches Q2 R2 S2	05/06/1915	10/06/1915
War Diary	Rue Du Quesne	11/06/1915	16/06/1915
War Diary	In Trenches R2 S2 P3	17/06/1915	22/06/1915
War Diary	Rue Du Quesne	23/06/1915	25/06/1915
War Diary	Sailly	26/06/1915	26/06/1915
War Diary	Dulieu	27/06/1915	28/06/1915
War Diary	Vicinity of Fletre	29/06/1915	29/06/1915
War Diary	Proven	30/06/1915	30/06/1915
Heading	146th Inf. Bde 49th Div. 1/7th Battn. The West Yorkshire Regiment. July 1915		
War Diary	Proven	01/07/1915	06/07/1915
War Diary	Yeres N. Salient	07/07/1915	14/07/1915
War Diary	Brielen	15/07/1915	19/07/1915
War Diary	Ypres N Salient	20/07/1915	25/07/1915
War Diary	Yser Canal	26/07/1915	31/07/1915
Heading	146th Inf. Bde 49th Div. 1/7th Battn. The West Yorkshire Regiment. August 1915		
War Diary	Ypres N Salient	01/08/1915	06/08/1915
War Diary	Brielen	07/08/1915	12/08/1915
War Diary	Ypres. N Salient	13/08/1915	30/08/1915
War Diary	Elverdinghe	31/08/1915	31/08/1915
Heading	146th Inf. Bde. 49th Div. 1/7th Battn. The West Yorkshire Regiment. September 1915		
War Diary	Elverdinghe	01/09/1915	09/09/1915
War Diary	Copper Nollehoek	10/09/1915	19/09/1915
War Diary	Pilkem Trenches	20/09/1915	23/09/1915
War Diary	Support	24/09/1915	27/09/1915
War Diary	Pilkem Trenches	28/09/1915	30/09/1915
Heading	146th Inf. Bde. 49th Div. 1/7th Battn. The West Yorkshire Regiment October 1915		

War Diary	Pilckem Trenches	01/10/1915	01/10/1915
War Diary	In Support	02/10/1915	05/10/1915
War Diary	Pilckem Trenches	06/10/1915	09/10/1915
War Diary	In Support	10/10/1915	14/10/1915
War Diary	Copper Nollehoek	15/10/1915	27/10/1915
War Diary	Canal Bank in Support	28/10/1915	30/10/1915
War Diary	Trenches	31/10/1915	31/10/1915
War Diary	B.16-D.20	31/10/1915	31/10/1915
Heading	146th Inf. Bde. 49th Div. 1/7th Battn. The West Yorkshire Regiment November 1915		
War Diary	Trenches B.16-D.20	01/11/1915	05/11/1915
War Diary	Canal Bank Rt. Support	06/11/1915	07/11/1915
War Diary	Trenches B16-D.20	08/11/1915	11/11/1915
War Diary	Coppernollehoek Camp No 2	12/11/1915	19/11/1915
War Diary	Trenches D.21. D.22	20/11/1915	21/11/1915
War Diary	Support	22/11/1915	23/11/1915
War Diary	Trenches D.19 & 20	24/11/1915	27/11/1915
War Diary	In Divl. resve. Coppernollehoek Camp No. 2	28/11/1915	30/11/1915
Heading	146th Inf. Bde. 49th Div. 1/7th Battn. The West Yorkshire Regiment. December 1915		
War Diary	Coppernollehoek Camp No 2	01/12/1915	07/12/1915
War Diary	Trenches D.21 D.22	08/12/1915	11/12/1915
War Diary	Right Support	12/12/1915	13/12/1915
War Diary	Trenches D.19-20	14/12/1915	17/12/1915
War Diary	Right Support	18/12/1915	19/12/1915
War Diary	Trenches D.21 D.22	20/12/1915	23/12/1915
War Diary	Right Support	24/12/1915	25/12/1915
War Diary	Trenches D19. 20	26/12/1915	29/12/1915
War Diary	Camp. C (Ref. L.3 Sheet 27.)	30/12/1915	30/12/1915
War Diary	Houtkerque	31/12/1915	31/12/1915
Heading	1/7th W. Yorkshire Regt. Jan. Vol X.		
War Diary	Wormhoudt	01/01/1916	15/01/1916
War Diary	Merckeghem	16/01/1916	16/01/1916
War Diary	Zutkerque	17/01/1916	17/01/1916
War Diary	Calais	18/01/1916	31/01/1916
Heading	War Diary 1/7 West. Yorks. Rgt Feb 1916 Vol XI		
War Diary	Calais	01/02/1916	01/02/1916
War Diary	Longeau	02/02/1916	02/02/1916
War Diary	Fourdrinoy	03/02/1916	05/02/1916
War Diary	Picquigny	06/02/1916	10/02/1916
War Diary	Molliens-Au-Bois	11/02/1916	11/02/1916
War Diary	Bouzincourt	12/02/1916	12/02/1916
War Diary	In Support Authville	13/02/1916	20/02/1916
War Diary	In Trenches G.2	21/02/1916	24/02/1916
War Diary	Martinsart	25/02/1916	29/02/1916
Heading	1/7 W York Regt Vol XII March 1916		
War Diary	In Trenches G.2. Section	01/03/1916	05/03/1916
War Diary	Bouzincourt	06/03/1916	06/03/1916
War Diary	Harponville	07/03/1916	14/03/1916
War Diary	Frechencourt	15/03/1916	31/03/1916
Heading	1/7 W York Regt Vol XIII April 1916		
War Diary	Frechencourt	01/04/1916	08/04/1916
War Diary	Vignacourt	09/04/1916	25/04/1916
War Diary	Flixecourt	26/04/1916	23/05/1916
War Diary	Vignacourt	24/05/1916	28/05/1916
War Diary	On March	29/05/1916	31/05/1916

Heading	146th Brigade. 49th Division. 1/7th Battalion West Yorkshire Regiment. June 1916		
War Diary	Aveluy Wood	01/06/1916	19/06/1916
War Diary	Hedauville Wood	20/06/1916	22/06/1916
War Diary	Puchevillers	23/06/1916	27/06/1916
War Diary	Varennes	28/06/1916	30/06/1916
Heading	146th Inf. Bde. 49th Div. War Diary 1/7th Battn. The West Yorkshire Regiment. July 1916		
War Diary	Aveluy Wood	01/07/1916	01/07/1916
War Diary	Thiepval Wood	01/07/1916	02/07/1916
War Diary	Aveluy Wood	03/07/1916	03/07/1916
War Diary	Martinsart Wood	04/07/1916	07/07/1916
War Diary	Aveluy Wood	08/07/1916	08/07/1916
War Diary	Leipsig Salient	09/07/1916	09/07/1916
War Diary	S. Bluff Authville	10/07/1916	12/07/1916
War Diary	Leipsig Salient	13/07/1916	14/07/1916
War Diary	S. Bluff Authville	15/07/1916	16/07/1916
War Diary	Campbell Post	17/07/1916	21/07/1916
War Diary	Martinsart Wood	22/07/1916	24/07/1916
War Diary	Forceville	25/07/1916	31/07/1916
Heading	146th Brigade 49th Division 1/7th Battalion West Yorkshire Regiment. August 1916		
War Diary	Forceville	01/08/1916	03/08/1916
War Diary	Leipsigsalt.	04/08/1916	07/08/1916
War Diary	S. Bluff Authville	08/08/1916	10/08/1916
War Diary	Leipsig Salient	11/08/1916	13/08/1916
War Diary	S. Bluff	14/08/1916	18/08/1916
War Diary	Acheux Wood	19/08/1916	26/08/1916
War Diary	Tohnstones Port	27/08/1916	28/08/1916
War Diary	Martinsart Wood	29/08/1916	31/08/1916
Heading	146th Infantry Brigade. 49th. Division. 1/7th. West Yorkshire Regt. September 1916		
War Diary	Martin Sart Wood	01/09/1916	02/09/1916
War Diary	Aveluy Wood	03/09/1916	03/09/1916
War Diary	Thiepval Wood	04/09/1916	04/09/1916
War Diary	Martin Sart Wood	05/09/1916	07/09/1916
War Diary	Forceville	08/09/1916	18/09/1916
War Diary	Hedauville	19/09/1916	20/09/1916
War Diary	Johnstones Port	21/09/1916	27/09/1916
War Diary	Mailly Maillet Wood	28/09/1916	29/09/1916
War Diary	Raincheval	30/09/1916	30/09/1916
War Diary	Halloy	01/10/1916	01/10/1916
War Diary	Coulle Mont	02/10/1916	04/10/1916
War Diary	Sombrin	05/10/1916	10/10/1916
War Diary	Humber Camps	11/10/1916	18/10/1916
War Diary	Fonquevillers	19/10/1916	24/10/1916
War Diary	Bienvillers	25/10/1916	02/11/1916
War Diary	Fonquevillers	03/11/1916	08/11/1916
War Diary	St Amand	09/11/1916	14/11/1916
War Diary	Fonquevillers	15/11/1916	20/11/1916
War Diary	Bienvillers	21/11/1916	30/11/1916
War Diary	Fonquevillers	01/12/1916	02/12/1916
War Diary	Souastre	03/12/1916	03/12/1916
War Diary	Bouquemaison	04/12/1916	31/12/1916
Heading	War Diary of 1/7th Batt West Yorks Regt for January 1917. Vol 22		

Heading	War Diary of for 1917		
Miscellaneous	49th (West Riding) Division No A/69/3	12/01/1917	12/01/1917
War Diary	Bouquemaison	01/01/1917	06/01/1917
War Diary	Bailleulmont G.2 Section.	07/01/1917	11/01/1917
War Diary	Bailleulval	12/01/1917	14/01/1917
War Diary	C.2 Sector	15/01/1917	19/01/1917
War Diary	Bailleulmont	20/01/1917	23/01/1917
War Diary	C.2 Sector	24/01/1917	27/01/1917
War Diary	Bailleulval	28/01/1917	31/01/1917
Heading	War Diary of 1/7th Batt West York Regt. for February 1917		
War Diary	C 2 Sector	01/02/1917	02/02/1917
War Diary	Humber Camp	03/02/1917	07/02/1917
War Diary	C.2 Sector	08/02/1917	11/02/1917
War Diary	Bailleulmont	12/02/1917	15/02/1917
War Diary	C.2 Sector	16/02/1917	21/02/1917
War Diary	Bailleulmont	22/02/1917	22/02/1917
War Diary	Ivergny	23/02/1917	24/02/1917
War Diary	Bouquemaison	25/02/1917	25/02/1917
War Diary	Croisette	26/02/1917	26/02/1917
War Diary	Cauchy A La Tour	27/02/1917	27/02/1917
War Diary	St. Venant	28/02/1917	28/02/1917
War Diary	Lestrem	01/03/1917	01/03/1917
War Diary	Levantie	02/03/1917	07/03/1917
War Diary	Fauquisart R. Sub Sector.	08/03/1917	13/03/1917
War Diary	Red House	14/03/1917	19/03/1917
War Diary	Fauquisart R. Sub Sector.	20/03/1917	25/03/1917
War Diary	Levantie	26/03/1917	31/03/1917
Heading	War Diary of 1/7th Batt West York Regt. for April 1917. Vol 25		
War Diary	Fauquisart Right Section	01/04/1917	05/04/1917
War Diary	Red House	06/04/1917	12/04/1917
War Diary	Fauquisart Right Sub Section	13/04/1917	18/04/1917
War Diary	Laventie	19/04/1917	24/04/1917
War Diary	Right Sub Sector Fauquisart	25/04/1917	30/04/1917
War Diary	Red House Laventie	01/05/1917	06/05/1917
War Diary	Right Sub Sector Fauquisart	06/05/1917	11/05/1917
War Diary	La Gorgue	12/05/1917	18/05/1917
War Diary	Reo House Laventie	19/05/1917	24/05/1917
War Diary	Laventie	25/05/1917	30/05/1917
War Diary	Right Sub Sector Fauquisart Sector	31/05/1917	31/05/1917
Heading	War Diary of 1/7th Batt West Yorks Regt for June 1917. Vol 27		
War Diary	Right Sub Sector Fauquisart Sector	01/06/1917	05/06/1917
War Diary	La Gorgue	06/06/1917	13/06/1917
War Diary	Laventie	14/06/1917	17/06/1917
War Diary	Fauquisart	18/06/1917	30/06/1917
Heading	War Diary of 1/7th Batt. West York Regt for July 1917. Vol 28		
War Diary	Right Sub Sector Fauquisart	01/07/1917	01/07/1917
War Diary	Laventie	06/07/1917	10/07/1917
War Diary	Estaires	11/07/1917	13/07/1917
War Diary	Mardyk Camp	14/07/1917	16/07/1917
War Diary	Fort De Dunes	17/07/1917	17/07/1917
War Diary	Coxyde	18/07/1917	18/07/1917
War Diary	Ribaillet Camp	19/07/1917	25/07/1917

War Diary	Left Sub Sector St. Georges Sector	26/07/1917	31/07/1917
Heading	War Diary of 1/7th Batt West York Regt for August 1917. Vol 29		
War Diary	Left Sub-Sector St. Georges Sector.	01/08/1917	01/08/1917
War Diary	Oost Dunkerke	02/08/1917	02/08/1917
War Diary	Ghyvelde	03/08/1917	03/08/1917
War Diary	Teteghem	04/08/1917	27/08/1917
War Diary	Ghyvelde	28/08/1917	31/08/1917
Heading	War Diary of 1/7th Batt West York Regt for September 1917. Vol 30		
War Diary	Ghyvelde	01/09/1917	24/09/1917
War Diary	Teteghem	25/09/1917	25/09/1917
War Diary	Wormhoudt	26/09/1917	26/09/1917
War Diary	Ochtezeele	27/09/1917	28/09/1917
War Diary	Longuenesse	29/09/1917	30/09/1917
Heading	War Diary of 1/7 Bn West York Rgt for 1st to 31st October 1917. Vol 31		
War Diary	Longueness	01/10/1917	01/10/1917
War Diary	Terdeghem	02/10/1917	03/10/1917
War Diary	Shrine Camp	04/10/1917	04/10/1917
War Diary	Watou	05/10/1917	06/10/1917
War Diary	Vlamertinghe	07/10/1917	08/10/1917
War Diary	Bricke	08/10/1917	08/10/1917
War Diary	Calgary Grange	09/10/1917	11/10/1917
War Diary	Nieltje	11/10/1917	11/10/1917
War Diary	Vlamertinghe	12/10/1917	12/10/1917
War Diary	Oudezeele	13/10/1917	28/10/1917
War Diary	East Steenyoorde	29/10/1917	31/10/1917
Miscellaneous	Narrative of Recent Operation.	13/10/1917	13/10/1917
Map	Message Map.		
Miscellaneous	Message Form.		
Heading	War Diary of 1/7th Battalion (P.W.O) West Yorkshire Regiment (T.F) from Nov 1st 1917 to Nov 30th 1917. Vol 32		
War Diary	East Steenyoorde Area	01/11/1917	07/11/1917
War Diary	Ypres	08/11/1917	11/11/1917
War Diary	West Hoek Sector	12/11/1917	15/11/1917
War Diary	Anzac Ridge Westhoek	16/11/1917	19/11/1917
War Diary	Swan Area W.of Ypres	20/11/1917	20/11/1917
War Diary	Dickebusch	21/11/1917	24/11/1917
War Diary	Halifax Camp	25/11/1917	28/11/1917
War Diary	Potijze	29/11/1917	30/11/1917
Heading	War Diary Of 1/7 Bn W. York Regt from Dec 1st 1917 to Dec 3rd 1917. Vol 33		
War Diary	Potijze	01/12/1917	05/12/1917
War Diary	Westhoek Sector	06/12/1917	08/12/1917
War Diary	Garter Point	09/12/1917	11/12/1917
War Diary	Canal Area Near Ypres	12/12/1917	17/12/1917
War Diary	Left Sub Sector Veer FME.	18/12/1917	23/12/1917
War Diary	Anzac House	24/12/1917	29/12/1917
War Diary	Potijze	30/12/1917	30/12/1917
War Diary	Vancouver Camp	31/12/1917	31/12/1917
Heading	War Diary of 1/7th Bn. West Yorkshire Regt. from 1-1-18 to 31-1-18		
War Diary	Vancouver Camp	01/01/1918	08/01/1918
War Diary	Dragoon Camp	09/01/1918	13/01/1918

War Diary	Staple	14/01/1918	31/01/1918
Heading	War Diary 1/7th Batt (P.W.O) West Yorkshire Regt 1/2/18-28/2/18. Vol 35		
War Diary	Staple	01/02/1918	01/02/1918
War Diary	Houlle	02/02/1918	05/02/1918
War Diary	Staple	06/02/1918	11/02/1918
War Diary	Montreal Camp Brandhoek	12/02/1918	28/02/1918
Miscellaneous	Attempted Enemy Raid on the trenches held by the 1/7 W.York Rgt. on the Brood Seinde Ridge on the night of the 23rd/24th Feby 1918	23/02/1918	23/02/1918
Heading	War Diary of 1/7th Bn. (P.W.O.) W. York. Rgt. 1/3/18-31/3/18. Vol 36		
War Diary	Garter Point	01/03/1918	03/03/1918
War Diary	Hussar Camp	04/03/1918	04/03/1918
War Diary	Potijze	05/03/1918	07/03/1918
War Diary	Left Sector Broodseinde Rdge.	08/03/1918	11/03/1918
War Diary	Garter Point	12/03/1918	15/03/1918
War Diary	Huzzar Camp	16/03/1918	18/03/1918
War Diary	Potijze	18/03/1918	19/03/1918
War Diary	Left Sector Broodseinde Ridge	20/03/1918	23/03/1918
War Diary	Garter Pt.	24/03/1918	27/03/1918
War Diary	Molenaarelsthoek	28/03/1918	30/03/1918
War Diary	West Farm Camp	31/03/1918	31/03/1918
Heading	146th Brigade. 49th Division. 1/7th Battalion West Yorkshire Regiment April 1918. Attached:- Report on Operations 10th-16th April 1918		
War Diary	West Farm Camp	01/04/1918	01/04/1918
War Diary	Tower Hamlets	02/04/1918	05/04/1918
War Diary	Tor Top	06/04/1918	06/04/1918
War Diary	Cameron Sector	07/04/1918	09/04/1918
War Diary	Lankhof Camp	10/04/1918	10/04/1918
War Diary	Chippewa Camp	10/04/1918	10/04/1918
War Diary	Lincoln Camp	11/04/1918	11/04/1918
War Diary	Wytchaete	12/04/1918	18/04/1918
War Diary	Farm in N.8.B.	19/04/1918	25/04/1918
War Diary	Ouderdom	26/04/1918	27/04/1918
War Diary	Hoograaf Cabt.	28/04/1918	28/04/1918
War Diary	Farm in K.23.b	29/04/1918	30/04/1918
Miscellaneous	62nd Infantry Brigade.	20/04/1918	20/04/1918
Heading	War Diary of 1/7th Battn. P.W.O (West Yorkshire) Regt. 1/5/18-31/5/18. Vol 38		
War Diary	Farm in K.23 (Sheet 27)	01/05/1918	05/05/1918
War Diary	St. Jan Ter Biezen	06/05/1918	25/05/1918
War Diary	Cormette	26/05/1918	31/05/1918
Heading	War Diary of 1/7th Bn. P.W.O. (W York Rgt) 1/6/18-30/6/18. Vol 39		
War Diary	Proven	01/06/1918	03/06/1918
War Diary	Brake Camp	04/06/1918	11/06/1918
War Diary	Ypres	12/06/1918	29/06/1918
War Diary	Siege Camp	30/06/1918	30/06/1918
Heading	War Diary of 1/7th Bn. P.W.O. (West Yorkshire Regt) T.F. July 1st-31st 1918. Vol 40		
War Diary	Siege Camp	01/07/1918	07/07/1918
War Diary	Bde Reserve S of Ypres	08/07/1918	15/07/1918
War Diary	Zillebeke Sector	16/07/1918	22/07/1918
War Diary	Brown Line	23/07/1918	23/07/1918

War Diary	Orillia Camp	24/07/1918	31/07/1918
Heading	War Diary 1/7th Battn. P.W.O. (West Yorkshire Rgt.T.F.) 1/8/18-31/8/18. Vol 41		
War Diary	Ypres	01/08/1918	16/08/1918
War Diary	Brake Camp A.30 Central Sheet 28	17/08/1918	18/08/1918
War Diary	Proven	19/08/1918	19/08/1918
War Diary	Herzeele	20/08/1918	22/08/1918
War Diary	Zutkerque	23/08/1918	23/08/1918
War Diary	La Panne	24/08/1918	28/08/1918
War Diary	Ternas	29/08/1918	31/08/1918
Heading	7 West Yorkshire Regiment War Diary September 1918. Vol 42		
War Diary	Ternas	01/09/1918	01/09/1918
War Diary	Me St Eloy	02/09/1918	11/09/1918
War Diary	Rly Embankment	12/09/1918	12/09/1918
War Diary	Plouvain	13/09/1918	16/09/1918
War Diary	Rly	17/09/1918	20/09/1918
War Diary	Plouvain Sector	21/09/1918	21/09/1918
War Diary	Cam Valley	21/09/1918	23/09/1918
War Diary	Arras	24/09/1918	30/09/1918
Heading	1/7th Bn. P.W.O. (West Yorkshire Regt.) War Diary October 1918. Vol 43. H.Q. 14th Inf. Bde.		
War Diary	Arras	01/10/1918	07/10/1918
War Diary	Cagnicourt	08/10/1918	09/10/1918
War Diary	Raillencourt	10/10/1918	11/10/1918
War Diary	Iwuy Area	11/10/1918	12/10/1918
War Diary	Avesnes-Le-Sec. Area	13/10/1918	14/10/1918
War Diary	Villers-En-Cauchies	15/10/1918	17/10/1918
War Diary	Escaudoeuvres	18/10/1918	20/10/1918
War Diary	Iwuy	21/10/1918	27/10/1918
War Diary	Noyelles	28/10/1918	31/10/1918
Miscellaneous	Diary of Action E of Cambrai on Oct. 11th 1918	17/10/1918	17/10/1918
Heading	War Diary of 1/7th Battn. P.W.O (West Yorkshire Rgt.) T.F. 1/11/18-30/11/18		
War Diary	Famars	01/11/1918	01/11/1918
War Diary	Aulnoy	02/11/1918	02/11/1918
War Diary	Famars	02/11/1918	02/11/1918
War Diary	Lieu St. Amand	03/11/1918	05/11/1918
War Diary	Evin Malmaison	06/11/1918	30/11/1918
Miscellaneous	War Diary of Operation on November 1st. 1918	01/11/1918	01/11/1918
Miscellaneous	The following Officers took part in this operation.		
Miscellaneous	Copy of message received from Corps Commander, XXII Corps.	02/11/1918	02/11/1918
Heading	War Diary of 1/7th Bn P.W.O. (West Yorkshire Regt.) December 1st 1918 to 31st 1918. Vol 45		
War Diary	Evin Malmaison	01/12/1918	31/12/1918
Miscellaneous	Enclosure to Special Order of the day. by Major General N.J.G. Cameron, C.B., C.M.G., Commanding 49th (West Riding) Division.	18/12/1918	18/12/1918
Miscellaneous	Special Order of the day by Major General N.J.G. Cameron, C.R., C.M.G., Commanding 49th (West Riding) Division.	18/12/1918	18/12/1918
Heading	War Diary of 1/7th Battn. P.W.O (West Yorkshire Rgt. T.F.) 1/1/19-31/1/19 Vol 46		
War Diary	Evin Malmaison	01/01/1919	16/01/1919
War Diary	Loos	17/01/1919	17/01/1919

War Diary	Evin Malmaison	18/01/1919	28/02/1919
Heading	War Diary of 1/7th Batt. P.W.O (West Yorkshire Regiment) 1-3-19-310319. Vol 48		
War Diary	Evin Malmaison	01/03/1919	03/03/1919
War Diary	Douai	04/03/1919	31/03/1919
Heading	War Diary of 1/7th West Yorkshire Rgt. 1/4/19-30/4/19. Vol 49		
War Diary	Douai	01/04/1919	30/04/1919
Heading	War Diary of 1/7th Battn P.W.O. (West Yorkshire Rgt T.E.) 1/5/19-31/5/19. Vol 50		
War Diary	Douai	01/05/1919	31/05/1919

WO95/2795/1

1/7 Battalion West Yorkshire Regiment

49TH DIVISION
146TH INFY BDE

1-7TH BN WEST YORKS REGT.
APR 1915-MAY 1919

146th Inf.Bde.
49th Div.

Battn. disembarked
Boulogne from
England 16.4.15.

1/7th BATTN. THE WEST YORKSHIRE REGIMENT.

A P R I L

(16/30.4.15)

1 9 1 5

May '19

Army Form C. 2118.

1/7th West York

WAR DIARY
or
INTELLIGENCE SUMMARY.
(Erase heading not required.)

Instructions regarding War Diaries and Intelligence Summaries are contained in F. S. Regs., Part II. and the Staff Manual respectively. Title pages will be prepared in manuscript.

Place	Date	Hour	Summary of Events and Information	Remarks and references to Appendices
BOULOGNE	April 16	2.15 AM	Arrived in camp at OSTROHOVE after unsuccessful passage from FOLKESTONE.	Pont de Briques Station.
		7.15 PM	Left Boulogne by train conveying one Transport which disembarked at HAVRE.	
MERVILLE	April 17	2.10 AM	Arrived at MERVILLE and proceeded to Temporary Billets in the Town. One man fell from train near ST OMER.	No 1815 Rgm L. CLAYDEN
		9. PM	Marched out to allotted Billeting Area.	
		6.15 PM	Battalion in close billets, mostly Farm houses. Very scattered.	
MERVILLE	April 18th		Nothing of importance happened	
MERVILLE	April 19th	6.30 PM	No 1815 Rgm L. CLAYDEN rejoined the Battalion unharmed.	
		7.0 PM	21 Officers & NCOs went into Trenches occupied by 2nd BEDFORDSHIRE Regt for instruction.	
MERVILLE	20th	7 PM	21 Officers + NCOs went into Trenches occupied by 2nd BEDFORDSHIRE Regt for instruction	
MERVILLE	21st	7 PM	25 Officers & NCOs relieved those who were under instruction on 24th going in with 4/GRENADIER GDS	
MERVILLE	22nd	4.30 PM	Moved to Vicinity of LA GORGUE, into close billets, just N of Village	
West LA GORGUE	23rd		Nothing of note	

Army Form C. 2118.

WAR DIARY 1/7th West York
or
INTELLIGENCE SUMMARY.

(Erase heading not required.)

Place	Date	Hour	Summary of Events and Information	Remarks and references to Appendices
N of La Gorgue	April 24	PM 7.30	4 Platoons to trenches with BORDER REG.T The Battalion temporarily attached to 21st Bde (B. Gen H E Watts C.B. C.M.G) for tactical work.	Sgt
		9	The above order cancelled, the Platoons returned to billets.	Sgt
N of La Gorgue	25th	PM 5	2 platoons to trenches with 2nd Gordon Highrs	Sgt
N of La Gorgue	26th	PM 5	2 platoons to trenches with 2nd Gordon Highrs	Sgt
N of La Gorgue	27th	PM 4	6 platoons to trenches (4 to 1st G.G. 2 to 6th Gordons)	Sgt
		4.30	Above cancelled 4 platoons only proceeding to trenches to 1st G Gds.	
N of La Gorgue	28th	PM 4.30	6 platoons to trenches 4 to 2nd BORDER Regt. 2 to 2nd Scots Gds.	Sgt
N of La Gorgue	29th	—	Nothing to report.	Sgt
N of La Gorgue	30th	—	Nothing to report. Orders received to hold battalion party in readiness to proceed to BAC ST MAUR on May 1st.	Sgt

146th Inf.Bde.
49th Div.

1/7th BATTN. THE WEST YORKSHIRE REGIMENT.

M A Y

1 9 1 5

Army Form C. 2118.

WAR DIARY
or
INTELLIGENCE SUMMARY.

1/7th West Yorks

(Erase heading not required.)

Instructions regarding War Diaries and Intelligence Summaries are contained in F. S. Regs., Part II. and the Staff Manual respectively. Title pages will be prepared in manuscript.

Place	Date	Hour	Summary of Events and Information	Remarks and references to Appendices
Hd Qu La Gorgue	May 1st	A.M. 6.15	Orders received to stand by for immediate move.	Sig/Capt
		10.35	Above order cancelled, normal conditions resumed, Billeting party to proceed as before.	Sig/Capt
Bac St Maur	2nd	12 noon	Arrived in Billets at Bac St Maur. The Brigade in Divisional Reserve.	Sig/Capt
Bac St Maur	3rd		Nothing of note happened.	Sig/Capt
Bac St Maur	4th		Nothing of note happened.	Sig/Capt
Bac St Maur	5th	P.M. 2	Brigade left for Laventie. The Battalion relieves the 2/Scots Guards in D lines Trenches at 10 p.m.	Sig/Capt
In Trenches "D" lines	6th		Nothing of importance happened.	Sig/Capt 1 Grundy No 2904 Rfm Holden killed
In Trenches "D" lines	7th		Nothing of importance happened	Sig/Capt 3 killed 1 wound

Army Form C. 2118.

1/4th Wee Yorkshire (A.)

WAR DIARY
or
INTELLIGENCE SUMMARY.
(Erase heading not required.)

Instructions regarding War Diaries and Intelligence Summaries are contained in F. S. Regs., Part II. and the Staff Manual respectively. Title pages will be prepared in manuscript.

Place	Date	Hour	Summary of Events and Information	Remarks and references to Appendices
In Trenches D Lines	MAY 8TH		Nothing of importance happened	Sig/Cpt 2 men wounded.
In Trenches D Lines	9TH	AM 5.0	Bombardment commenced. Parapets suffered from our own Artillery and from Hostile artillery.	Sig/Cpt 3 Killed & 9 wounded.
			Bombardment continued all day.	
		PM 4.0	Terrific bombardment to S in region of Bois de Biez, remote towards dusk.	Sig/Cpt
		8 PM	Artillery firing all along line. Situation quiet to our immediate front.	Sig/Cpt
In Trenches D Lines	10TH		Nothing of importance happened. Artillery duel.	Sig/Cpt 1 Killed
In Trenches D Lines	11TH		Nothing of importance happened. Artillery destroyed house said to contain machine guns which were worrying our ration parties at night.	Sig/Cpt
In Trenches D Lines	12TH		Nothing of importance happened.	Sig/Cpt
In Trenches D Lines	13TH		Nothing of importance happened.	Sig/Cpt 1 Killed.
In Trenches D Lines	14TH		Nothing of importance happened.	Sig/Cpt 1 Killed.
In Trenches D Lines	15TH	10 PM	Nothing of importance happened. Relieved in Trenches by 1/London Regt.	Sig/Cpt 1 Killed

Army Form C. 2118.

WAR DIARY
or
INTELLIGENCE SUMMARY.
(Erase heading not required.)

(5)

Instructions regarding War Diaries and Intelligence Summaries are contained in F. S. Regs., Part II. and the Staff Manual respectively. Title pages will be prepared in manuscript.

Place	Date	Hour	Summary of Events and Information	Remarks and references to Appendices
Bac St Maur	May 16th	AM 9	Int billets near Bac St Maur (Rue de Bruges)	Sgt/Capt
—	17th		Nothing of importance happened.	Sgt/Capt
—	18th	PM 6.15	Vacated billets and took over that of 1/6 P.I. at same time rejoining 49th (W.R.) Divn	Sgt/Capt
Rue du Quesne	19th	9.0	In billets in Rue du Quesne	Sgt/Capt
—	20th		Nothing of importance happened.	Sgt/Capt
—	21st	PM 8	Took over line of trenches Q2, R2, S2, and forts D2 and E2 from 1/5th West Yorkshire Regt.	Sgt/Capt
In Trenches Q2, R2, S2	22nd		Nothing of importance happened	Sgt/Capt
—	23rd		Nothing of importance happened. More firing on the part of the enemy than usual.	Sgt/Capt 2 Killed. 2 Wounded.
—	24th	PM 8	Bombardment commenced	Sgt/Capt
		9	Bombardment ceased	Sgt/Capt
	25th	Midnight 12.10 AM	Bombardment re-opened	Sgt/Capt 2 Killed.
			Bombardment ceased	
		3.20 PM	Bombardment re-opened	tactical points near
		3.27 PM	Bombardment ceased	148th Bde advanced and captured German 1st line of trenches. Nothing of importance happened opposite our lines.
		9 AM	Short bombardment	tactical points
		12 Noon	Short bombardment	148th Bde made good front line of German trenches with flanking patrols established.
				Sgt/Capt 3/G.W.S.Y. Kes Killed in trenches.
—	26th		Nothing of importance happened	Sgt/Capt

1577 Wt. W10791/1773 500,000 1/15 D. D. & L. A.D.S.S./Forms/C. 2118.

Army Form C. 2118.

WAR DIARY
or
INTELLIGENCE SUMMARY.
(Erase heading not required.)

Instructions regarding War Diaries and Intelligence Summaries are contained in F. S. Regs., Part II. and the Staff Manual respectively. Title pages will be prepared in manuscript.

(6)

Place	Date	Hour	Summary of Events and Information	Remarks and references to Appendices
In Trenches	May			
R₂ R₂ S₂	27ᵗʰ		Nothing of importance happened	Knyfft Capt
—	28ᵗʰ		Nothing of importance happened. A shell somewhat heavy - 2 men wounded, no other damage done.	Knyfft Capt
—	29ᵗʰ	8 PM	Relieved in trenches by 1/6ᵗʰ West Yorkshire Regt. Taking over billets vacated by them in Rue du Quesne.	Knyfft Capt
Rue du Quesne	30ᵗʰ		Nothing of importance happened.	Knyfft Capt
—	31ˢᵗ		Nothing of importance happened.	Knyfft Capt

1577 Wt.W10791/1773 500,000 1/15 D. D. & L. A.D.S.S./Forms/C. 2118.

146th Inf.Bde.
49th Div.

1/7th BATTN. THE WEST YORKSHIRE REGIMENT.

J U N E

1 9 1 5

WAR DIARY
or
INTELLIGENCE SUMMARY.

(Erase heading not required.)

Army Form C. 2118.

Instructions regarding War Diaries and Intelligence Summaries are contained in F.S. Regs., Part II and the Staff Manual respectively. Title pages will be prepared in manuscript.

(7)

Place	Date	Hour	Summary of Events and Information	Remarks and references to Appendices
Rue du Quesne	June 1st		Nothing of note happened	Sgt Capt
" " "	2nd		Nothing of note happened	Sgt Capt
" " "	3rd		Nothing of note happened	Sgt Capt
" " "	4th	8pm	Nothing happened. Relieved A & 1/6th West Yorkshire Regt in the Trenches, who took over Billets in Rue du Quesne	Sgt Capt
In Trenches Q2, R2, S2	5th		Nothing of note happened	Sgt Capt
" " "	6th		Nothing of note happened	3rd Sgt Capt
" " "	7th		Nothing of note happened	Sgt Capt
" " "	8th		Nothing of note happened	Sgt Capt
" " "	9th		Nothing of note happened up to 9 pm	Sgt Capt
		9 pm	The enemy dropped several Trench mortar bombs into our lines doing considerable damage, killing 1 man and wounding 4. The Gallery	Sgt Capt
		10.15pm	were informed, and at 10.15 pm fired 6 rounds in or about the spot from which the bombs were fired, which silenced the mortar. The	
		1pm	accuracy of the Howitzer fire on a point so close to our own trenches elicited the men up no end.	
	10th	8.30	Relieved by Bn 1/6th West Yorkshire Regt in the Trenches, and took over their Billets in Rue du Quesne	Sgt Capt
Rue du Quesne	11th		Nothing of importance happened	Sgt Capt
" " "	12th		Nothing of importance happened	Sgt Capt
" " "	13th		Nothing of importance happened	Sgt Capt

WAR DIARY
or
INTELLIGENCE SUMMARY.

(Erase heading not required.)

Army Form C. 2118.

(8.)

Instructions regarding War Diaries and Intelligence Summaries are contained in F. S. Regs., Part II. and the Staff Manual respectively. Title pages will be prepared in manuscript.

Place	Date	Hour	Summary of Events and Information	Remarks and references to Appendices
	JUNE			
RUE du QUESNE	14th		Nothing of importance happened. Heavy shelling of artillery position	Knygtt Capt.
-"- -"-	15th		Nothing of importance happened. Heavy shelling of artillery position	Knygtt Capt.
-"- -"-	16th	8.30 P.M.	Battalion relieved 1/6th WEST YORKSHIRE REGt in sections Q2, R2, S2, + P3 & D2 and E2, 1/6th WEST YORKSHIRE REGt took our billets in RUE du QUESNE	Knygtt Capt.
In Trenches R2, S2, P3	17th		Nothing of importance happened.	Knygtt Capt.
-"- -"-	18th		Nothing happened. Sniper shelling duel. (1 wounded)	Knygtt Capt.
-"- -"-	19th		Nothing of importance happened. Cpl M Hoplin killed, Cpt SO Rabagan and 5 men wounded	Knygtt Capt.
-"- -"-	20th		Nothing of importance happened. Enemy artillery registered on our parapet.	Knygtt Capt.
-"- -"-	21st		Nothing of importance happened. Enemy artillery sheer Anti aircraft gun very heavily doing considerable damage	Knygtt Capt.
-"- -"-	22nd	8.30 P.M.	Relieved in trenches by 1/6th WEST YORKSHIRE REGt, and took over old billets in RUE du QUESNE	Knygtt Capt.
RUE du QUESNE	23rd		Nothing of importance happened.	Knygtt Capt.
-"- -"-	24th		Nothing of importance happened. Received orders to move South	Knygtt Capt.
-"- -"-	25th		Move to vicinity of SAILLY. advance party detailed for taking over new line. (TROU BAYARD, move South cancelled)	Knygtt Capt.
SAILLY	26th		Move to DULIEU	Knygtt Capt.
DULIEU	27th	9.00	Nothing happened of importance.	Knygtt Capt.
DULIEU	28th	8.15	Move to vicinity of FLETRE	Knygtt Capt.

Army Form C. 2118.

WAR DIARY
or
INTELLIGENCE SUMMARY.
(Erase heading not required.)

Instructions regarding War Diaries and Intelligence Summaries are contained in F.S. Regs., Part II. and the Staff Manual respectively. Title pages will be prepared in manuscript.

Place	Date	Hour	Summary of Events and Information	Remarks and references to Appendices
Vicinity of FLÊTRE	June 29th	9 pm	Moved to vicinity of PROVEN	Angt Capt
PROVEN	30th		In Billets and Bivouac	Angt Capt

146th Inf.Bde.
49th Div.

1/7th BATTN. THE WEST YORKSHIRE REGIMENT.

J U L Y

1 9 1 5

Army Form C. 2118.

WAR DIARY
or
INTELLIGENCE SUMMARY.
(Erase heading not required.)

Instructions regarding War Diaries and Intelligence Summaries are contained in F. S. Regs., Part II. and the Staff Manual respectively. Title pages will be prepared in manuscript.

Place	Date	Hour	Summary of Events and Information	Remarks and references to Appendices
PROVEN	JULY 1st		Inspected by Commander of 2nd Army	Sh/gh Capt.
—	2nd		Inspected by Commander of VI Corps	Sh/gh Capt.
—	3rd		Nothing of importance happened	Sh/gh Capt.
—	4th		Nothing of importance happened	Sh/gh Capt.
—	5th		Nothing of importance happened	Sh/gh Capt.
—	6th	6.30 pm	Moved to Duicurie N of POPERINGHE on way to take up new line of Trenches N of YPRES	Sh/gh Capt.
YPRES N. SALIENT	7th	10 pm	Moved off towards Trenches	Sh/gh Capt.
—	8th	1.45 am	Relief completed during heavy counter attack by Germans on Trenches S of PILKEM (½ mile N of our line)	Sh/gh Capt.
—	9th	5 pm	Heavy bombardment of rifle line. Gas shells used. 14 men sent to hospital suffering from effects of gas. Several men wounded by splinters of shells. Gas hung about Trenches for a considerable time.	Sh/gh Capt.
—	10th		Bombardment of rifle line, varying in severity throughout the day and night	Sh/gh Capt.
—	11th		Bombardment of rifle line, varying in severity throughout the day and night	Sh/gh Capt.
—	12th		Bombardment of rifle line, varying in severity throughout the day and night	Sh/gh Capt.
—	13th	7.30 pm 10.30	Severe bombardment of rifle line with mixed projectiles including gas shells. Relief postponed for considerable time	Sh/gh Capt.
—	14th	2.20 am	Relieved by 1/8 WEST YORKSHIRE Regt and marched to vicinity of BRIELEN	Sh/gh Capt.
BRIELEN	15th	12.30 10	Shelled by 6" Shrapnel — 1 officer + 7 men wounded. Moved into Dug outs behind CHATEAU vacated by 1/7 WEST RIDING Regt	Sh/gh Capt.

1577   Wt. W10791/1773   500,000   1/15   D. D. & L.   A.D.SS./Forms/C.2118.

Army Form C. 2118.

WAR DIARY
or
INTELLIGENCE SUMMARY.
(Erase heading not required.)

Instructions regarding War Diaries and Intelligence Summaries are contained in F. S. Regs., Part II. and the Staff Manual respectively. Title pages will be prepared in manuscript.

Place	Date	Hour	Summary of Events and Information	Remarks and references to Appendices
BRIELEN	JULY 16th		Nothing of importance happened. Divisional HQrs moved further back.	Rugby Capt.
---	17th		Chateau Shelled - Divisional Commander seeing rounds.	Rugby Capt.
---	18th		Nothing of importance happened	Rugby Capt.
---	19th	11 AM	Chateau shelled with Gas Shells.	Rugby Capt.
		10 PM	Relief of 1/8 WEST YORKSHIRE REGt commenced. Same frontiers as before.	Rugby Capt.
YPRES N SALIENT	20th	1 AM	Relief completed. Nothing of importance happened, customary bombardment of Trenches, more rifle fire than before	Rugby Capt.
---	21st		Customary shelling of Trenches	Rugby Capt.
---	22nd		Nothing to report. Customary shelling heavier than usual, rifle fire brisk	Rugby Capt.
---	23rd		Heavy shelling of Trenches - a few gas shells, rifle fire very brisk during night.	Rugby Capt.
---	24th		Customary shelling - no damage done or manuel.	Rugby Capt.
---	25th		Customary shelling.	Rugby Capt.
		7:15 PM	Saw German Aeroplane brought down by one of Allies fighting Planes	
		9	1/8th WEST YORKSHIRE REGt commenced relief	Rugby Capt.
		11:40	Relief Complete	Rugby Capt.
YSER CANAL	26th		Slight Shelling of Bridge, no damage done.	Rugby Capt.
---	27th		Bridge shelled, dam still intact.	Rugby Capt.

Army Form C. 2118.

WAR DIARY
or
~~INTELLIGENCE SUMMARY.~~
(Erase heading not required.)

Instructions regarding War Diaries and Intelligence Summaries are contained in F. S. Regs., Part II. and the Staff Manual respectively. Title pages will be prepared in manuscript.

Place	Date	Hour	Summary of Events and Information	Remarks and references to Appendices
YSER CANAL	JULY 28TH		Nothing of importance happens	Argyll Capt
—	29th	AM 9.30	Heavy shelling of dam commenced at rate of 2 8.27" H.E. shells for 5 minutes. This was kept up until 12 noon, when rate reduced to 1 per 5 minutes. Several Dug outs blown in. 1 Officer killed and 10 men wounded	Argyll Capt
—	30th	AM 1	Shelling ceased, only 2 shells fell after that hour — in all 230 odd shells fell near the dam — which remained untouched, although the adjoining bridge was damaged in 3 places. Nothing further of note happens	Argyll Capt
—	31st	AM 8.30	About 30 shells 8.27" H.E. fell near dam — no damage done.	Argyll Capt
—		PM 9.15	Start to relieve 1/8 WEST YORKSHIRE REGT in Trenches	

146th Inf.Bde.
49th Div.

1/7th BATTN. THE WEST YORKSHIRE REGIMENT.

A U G U S T

1 9 1 5

Army Form C. 2118.

WAR DIARY
or
INTELLIGENCE SUMMARY.
(Erase heading not required.)

Instructions regarding War Diaries and Intelligence Summaries are contained in F.S. Regs., Part II. and the Staff Manual respectively. Title pages will be prepared in manuscript.

Place	Date	Hour	Summary of Events and Information	Remarks and references to Appendices
YPRES N SALIENT	AUGUST 1st	AM 12.20	Relief complete. Took over Dugouts vacated by 1/8th West Yorkshire Regt at Chateau des Trois Tours #	Wright Capt
--	2nd		Nothing to report.	Wright Capt
--	3rd		Nothing to report.	Wright Capt
--	4th		Heavy bombardment of billet line by enemy — very little damage done	Wright Capt
--	5th		Heavy bombardment of billet line by enemy — very little damage done	Wright Capt
--	6th		Intense bombardment of billet line by enemy. Slight damage to dugouts and trench line	Wright Capt
--	7th		Relieved in Trenches by 1/8th West Yorkshire Regt	Wright Capt
BRIELEN	7th		Took over Dugouts vacated by 1/8th West Yorkshire Regt at Chateau des Trois Tours.	Wright Capt
--	8th		Bombardment of Enemy's line — Attack on Hooge front successful	Wright Capt
--	9th		Nothing to report	Wright Capt
--	10th		Nothing to report	Wright Capt
--	11th		Nothing to report	Wright Capt
--	12th		Nothing to report.	Wright Capt
YPRES N SALIENT	13th	AM 1.10	Relieved 1/8th West Yorkshire Regt in the Trenches	Wright Capt
--	14th		Nothing to report. Bombardment of front line by enemy — damage slight	Wright Capt
--	15th		Intermittent bombardment throughout day — damage slight	Wright Capt

1577 Wt W10791/1773 500,000 1/15 D. D. & L. A.D.S.S./Forms/C. 2118.

WAR DIARY
or
INTELLIGENCE SUMMARY

Army Form C. 2118.

Instructions regarding War Diaries and Intelligence Summaries are contained in F.S. Regs., Part II. and the Staff Manual respectively. Title pages will be prepared in manuscript.

(Erase heading not required.)

Place	Date	Hour	Summary of Events and Information	Remarks and references to Appendices
YPRES N SALIENT	August 16th	9 AM	Support Trenches shelled by enemy – no damage done.	Rugby Capt.
"	17th		Bombardment of enemy line by our Artillery. Retaliation by enemy poor.	Rugby Capt.
"	18th		Heavy trench mortars fire in our line – doing considerable damage – at 5 AM and 6 PM. Bombardment of Support Trenches throughout day.	Rugby Capt.
"	19th		Bombardment of High Command Trench by our Artillery. Retaliation by enemy very severe – but little damage done. Support Trenches heavily shelled by enemy.	Rugby Capt.
"	20th		Slight bombardment of our line by enemy.	Rugby Capt.
"	21st		Slight bombardment of our line by enemy.	Rugby Capt.
"	22		Nothing to report.	Rugby Capt.
"	23rd		Our trenches fired on by High Command Trench – Retaliation by enemy ineffective.	Rugby Capt.
"	24"		Heavy bombardment of our front line – damage slight.	Rugby Capt.
"	25th	6pm	Intense bombardment of front line. Trench mortars and heavy guns – damage severe.	Rugby Capt.
"	26th		Our howitzers shelled High Command Trench very effectively. Retaliation by enemy with H.E. & heavy calibre ineffective.	Rugby Capt.
"	27th	5pm	Machine gun bombardment of front line & Trench mortars & heavy guns – damage severe – no infantry attack followed.	Rugby Capt.
"	28th		Artillery duel.	Rugby Capt.
"	29th		Our Artillery accurately shelled High Command Trench doing much damage.	Rugby Capt.

Army Form C. 2118.

WAR DIARY
or
INTELLIGENCE SUMMARY.
(Erase heading not required.)

Place	Date	Hour	Summary of Events and Information	Remarks and references to Appendices
YPRES N SALIENT	AUGUST 30th		Nothing to report. Relieved in Trenches by 1/6th West Yorkshire Regt.	Night Capt.
EVERDINGHE	31st		Nothing to report.	Night Capt.

146th Inf.Bde.
49th Div.

1/7th BATTN. THE WEST YORKSHIRE REGIMENT.

S E P T E M B E R

1 9 1 5

Army Form C. 2118.

WAR DIARY
or
INTELLIGENCE SUMMARY.
(Erase heading not required.)

Instructions regarding War Diaries and Intelligence Summaries are contained in F. S. Regs., Part II. and the Staff Manual respectively. Title pages will be prepared in manuscript.

Place	Date	Hour	Summary of Events and Information	Remarks and references to Appendices
ELVERDINGHE	SEPT 1st		Rained.	Army Corps
-,,-	2nd	1.30 AM	Rained. Special Police duty to Officers 8 NCOs + 45 riflemen in Corps scheme in unauthorized prems.	Army Corps
-,,-	3rd	6 AM	Rained. Police relieved.	Army Corps
-,,-	4th		Rained.	Army Corps
-,,-	5th		Rained.	Army Corps
-,,-	6th		Nothing to report.	Army Corps
-,,-	7th		Saw new line of Trenches for defence (Artillery scheme).	Army Corps
-,,-	8th		Village shelled – About 16 shells fell in Chateau grounds – no damage done	Army Corps
-,,-	9th		Moved to vicinity of COPPERNOLLEHOEK	Army Corps
COPPERNOLLEHOEK	10th		Nothing to report. for 12 days rest.	Army Corps
-,,-	11th		Nothing to report. Inspected by Corps Commander	Army Corps
-,,-	12th		Nothing to report.	Army Corps
-,,-	13th		Nothing to report. Inspected by Army Commander	Army Corps
-,,-	14th		Nothing to report.	Army Corps
-,,-	15th		Nothing to report.	Army Corps
-,,-	16th		Nothing to report.	Army Corps
-,,-	17th		Nothing to report.	Army Corps
-,,-	18th		Nothing to report.	Army Corps
-,,-	19th		Took over PILKEM Line Trenches from 1/5th YORK + LANCASTER RegT	Army Corps
PILKEM TRENCHES	20th		Nothing to report.	Army Corps
-,,-	21st		Nothing to report.	Army Corps

Army Form C. 2118.

WAR DIARY
or
INTELLIGENCE SUMMARY.
(Erase heading not required.)

Instructions regarding War Diaries and Intelligence Summaries are contained in F. S. Regs., Part II. and the Staff Manual respectively. Title pages will be prepared in manuscript.

Place	Date Sept	Hour	Summary of Events and Information	Remarks and references to Appendices
PILKEM TRENCHES	22nd	PM 4-5	Slight bombardment of line	Knight Capt.
—	23rd	PM 9	Nothing to report. Relieved in Trenches by 1/6th WEST YORKSHIRE REGT	Knight Capt.
Support	24th		Nothing to report.	Knight Capt.
—	25th	AM 4	Bombardment of enemy line in conjunction with attack by movement further South	Knight Capt.
—	26th		Nothing to report	Knight Capt.
—	27th		Nothing of importance happened – Relieved 1/6th Bn in TRENCHES	Knight Capt.
PILKEM TRENCHES	28th		Slight bombardment during day – no damage done. Rained	Knight Capt.
—	29th		Nothing of importance happened – Very wet all day – Trenches in appalling state.	Knight Capt.
—	30th		Slight shelling of farms behind the line but practically all day Trenches flooded.	Knight Capt.

146th Inf.Bde.
49th Div.

1/7th BATTN. THE WEST YORKSHIRE REGIMENT.

O C T O B E R

1 9 1 5

Army Form C. 2118.

WAR DIARY
or
INTELLIGENCE SUMMARY.
(Erase heading not required.)

Instructions regarding War Diaries and Intelligence Summaries are contained in F. S. Regs., Part II. and the Staff Manual respectively. Title pages will be prepared in manuscript.

Place	Date	Hour	Summary of Events and Information	Remarks and references to Appendices
	Oct.			
Pickem Trenches	1st		Nothing of importance happened - rain. Relieved by 1/6 West Yorkshire Regt. after dark	Kingly Capt.
In Support	2nd		Nothing of importance happened.	Kingly Capt.
" "	3rd		Slight shelling of farms, no damage done.	Kingly Capt.
" "	4th		Nothing to report	Kingly Capt.
" "	5th		Rain, nothing of importance happened	Kingly Capt.
Pickem Trenches	6th	9.30 pm	Relieved the 1/6 West Yorkshire Regt. in the Trenches	Kingly Capt.
" "	7th	Noon	Talana Fm Shelled heavily - also Second Line. No casualties but a certain amount of damage done to stores.	Kingly Capt.
" "	"	7.30 pm	Talana Fm and Second Line shelled.	Kingly Capt.
" "	8th		Bombing duel in 1st Company (D)	Kingly Capt.
" "	"		Nothing of importance happened	Kingly Capt.
" "	9th	7-9 pm	Heavy shelling of Canal Bank - Talana Farm and Communication Trenches - Relief delayed 2 hours. Relieved in Trenches by 1/6th West Yorkshire Regt.	Kingly Capt.
In Support	10th		Nothing of importance happened	Kingly Capt.
" "	11th		Nothing of importance happened. Malakoff Fm Shelled. Orderly Room Staff knocked out. (6 wounded.)	Kingly Capt.
" "	12th		Nothing of importance happened.	Kingly Capt.
" "	13th	8-10 pm	Heavy shelling of all roads behind our lines. Bde relief delayed. Retaliation for our shelling during the afternoon of enemy front line and communication Trenches	Kingly Capt.

1577 Wt. W10791/1773 500,000 1/15 D. D. & L. A.D.S.S./Forms/C. 2118.

WAR DIARY
or
INTELLIGENCE SUMMARY
(Erase heading not required.)

Army Form C. 2118.

Instructions regarding War Diaries and Intelligence Summaries are contained in F. S. Regs., Part II. and the Staff Manual respectively. Title pages will be prepared in manuscript.

Place	Date	Hour	Summary of Events and Information	Remarks and references to Appendices
In Support	October 14th	9.45 pm	Nothing of importance happened. Relieved by 1/6th West Riding Regt	Knogsh Capt.
COPPERNOLLEHOEK	15th		Nothing of importance happened. M.G. Section relieved	Knogsh Capt.
—	16th		Inspections of Clothing Equipment etc all day - nothing of importance happened	Knogsh Capt.
—	17th		Inspections etc. Task & Browns nets - Huts and Shelters visited	Knogsh Capt.
—	18th		Inspections etc. ,, ,, ,, ,,	Knogsh Capt.
—	19th		Same as above. Every man in Battalion on a gift of socks	Knogsh Capt.
—	20th		Orders received to move to Trenches tomorrow. Road mending party under Capt TODD. Relieve portions of 148th Bde of 14th Division	Knogsh Capr.
—	21st	PM 11.15	Relieved 1/5th K.O.Y.L.I. in Trenches. D.21, D.22 a Support line FOCH T-W - LA BELLE ALLIANCE	Knogsh Capt.
—	22nd		Heavy bombardment of above line from 9am Till 4.30 pm little damage done	Knogsh Capt.
—	23rd		Quieter day - from 10 pm Till 1.30 am	Knogsh Capr.
—	24th	Noon	Enemy bombarded D.21, D.22 Trenches for 20 minutes, damage brought night. Rifle fire slack.	Knogsh Capt.
—	25th		A quiet day - FOCH TRENCH heavily shelled from Noon To 1.30 pm. otherwise a quiet day. Catch up with receipts of five hood and stores.	Knogsh Capt. 2ndy Off
—	26th		Communication Trenches shelled. GORBY STREET being knocked in in one place. Rifle fire slack.	Knogsh Capt.
—	27th		A quiet day. Relieved in the Trenches by 1/8th WEST YORKSHIRE REGT	Knogsh Capt.

Army Form C. 2118.

WAR DIARY
or
INTELLIGENCE SUMMARY

(Erase heading not required.)

Instructions regarding War Diaries and Intelligence Summaries are contained in F.S. Regs., Part II. and the Staff Manual respectively. Title pages will be prepared in manuscript.

Place	Date	Hour	Summary of Events and Information	Remarks and references to Appendices
	OCTOBER			
CANAL BANK in Support	28th		Rained all day. Battalion much scattered in Support line. Trenches and dugouts in very poor condition. Heavy bombardment all night.	Sgt y/o/c
"	29th		Rained - Trenches very bad - practically no work could be done. Heavy bombardment all afternoon.	Sgt y/Capt.
"	30th		4 APL Canal Bank shelled with Heavy stuff at 2.30 pm. Relieved 15th WEST YORKSHIRE REGT on right of Sector, Trenches B.16 to D.20.	Sgt y/Capt. 1 ATTACK KILLED
TRENCHES B.16–D.20	31st		Trenches in very bad condition - practically no work possible - all trenches under water. Rained.	Sgt y/Capt.

146th Inf.Bde.
49th Div.

1/7th BATTN. THE WEST YORKSHIRE REGIMENT.

NOVEMBER

1915

Army Form C. 2118.

WAR DIARY
or
INTELLIGENCE SUMMARY.
(Erase heading not required.)

Place	Date	Hour	Summary of Events and Information	Remarks and references to Appendices
TRENCHES B.16 - D.20	Nov R. 1st		Rained - Trenches falling in - too much for Companies to cope with - nearly 2 feet of water in all trenches	Rugby Capt.
- -	2nd		Rained. Trenches and dreams falling in - Dug outs continually collapsing - Equipment etc being buried beneath debris - impossible to locate when night landslides take place - water too deep.	Rugby Capt.
- -	3rd		Rained - Abandoned certain Trenches leaving post in front line to prevent any incursions. Boches from investigating position too minutely. Front abandoned covered by Machine Guns.	Rugby Capt.
- -	4th		Heavy Bombardment of YPRES district.	Rugby Capt.
- -	5th		Rained - relieved in Fr. Trenches by R. 1/8th WEST YORKSHIRE REGT.	Rugby Capt.
CANAL BANK R. Support	6th		Trenches taken over in bad condition - dispositions altered accordingly.	Rugby Capt.
- -	7th		Relieved 1/8th WEST YORKSHIRE REGT. in right of Sector B16 - D 20	Rugby Capt.
TRENCHES B/6 - D.20	8th		Trenches shelled at odd periods throughout the day mainly by WHIZZ-BANGS - little damage done.	Rugby Capt.
- -	9th		Trenches in rev g D 20 shelled with heavy stuff - Communication trench damaged in 2 places completely blocking the drains - Front line trenches getting much better.	Rugby Capt.
- -	10th		Rained. Nothing to report.	Rugby Capt.

1577 Wt.W10791/1773 500,000 1/15 D. D. & L. A.D.S.S./Forms/C. 2118.

Army Form C. 2118.

WAR DIARY
or
INTELLIGENCE SUMMARY.
(Erase heading not required.)

Instructions regarding War Diaries and Intelligence Summaries are contained in F. S. Regs., Part II. and the Staff Manual respectively. Title pages will be prepared in manuscript.

(22)

Place	Date	Hour	Summary of Events and Information	Remarks and references to Appendices
TRENCHES B.16-D.20	Nov. 11th		Wet. Trenches in bad condition - drainage very difficult being much hampered by bridges. Relieved by 1/8th Bn West Yorkshire Regt. Rain very bad in night.	Angst Capt
Coppernolhoek Camp No 2	12th		Camp in very bad condition - a quagmire. Companies got settled down in huts and after drawing 3 day Dry about in working things out.	Angst Capt
—	13th		Anything and putting up more huts carried on with. Mud very bad	Angst Capt
—	14th		Nothing could be done to the battlestand huts. Belgian workers about. Wooden huts carried on with. Working parties. 3 officers + 100 oth. ranks.	Angst Capt
—	15th		Huts still being put in material short. Working parties. German attack expected on Yser line. Rained.	Angst Capt
—	16th		No more material for huts. Huts put up to fact. for the R.E. Supply - Every available place in place. German attack expected on Yser line. Rained. Working parties. 1 officer + 100 oth ranks	Angst Capt
—	17th		Rained. Working party of 1 officer + 200 oth ranks	Angst Capt
—	18th		Place 2 Wattle + Daub huts rabbits. Working Party of 1 officer + 200 oth ranks	Angst Gen Angst Capt

Army Form C. 2118.

WAR DIARY
or
INTELLIGENCE SUMMARY.
(Erase heading not required.)

(23)

Instructions regarding War Diaries and Intelligence Summaries are contained in F. S. Regs., Part II. and the Staff Manual respectively. Title pages will be prepared in manuscript.

Place	Date	Hour	Summary of Events and Information	Remarks and references to Appendices
Coppernollehoek Camp No. 2.	Nov. 19th 1917		Relieved the 1/8th WEST YORKSHIRE REGT in the Trenches in LEFT SECTION. Battalion spread out as follows A+B Coys in D.21 + D.22, D Coy in DAWSON CITY, C Company W of PILCKEM ROAD. H.Q on CANAL BANK. 1/8th BN WEST YORKSHIRE REGT on our right.	Knight Capt.
Trenches D.21 D.22	20th		Hard frost. Trenches in bad condition, only possible method of visiting by night in the open. 1/8th WEST YORKSHIRE REGT on our right.	Knight Capt.
- -	21st		Relieved in the Trenches by 1/5th K.O.Y.L.I. Battalion spread out as follows:- D Company on W. side of CANAL BANK S of BRIDGE 4, C Company at HALF FARM, A+B Companies +H.Q at ELVERDINGHE CHATEAU called SUPPORT BATTALION	Knight Capt.
SUPPORT	22nd		Putting up tents and making overroom accomodation for 1/2 a Battalion. 2 working parties of (a) 1 officer + 50 or (b) 1 officer + 40 or	Knight Capt.
- -	23rd		Relieved the 1/5th BN. WEST YORKSHIRE REGT in the Trenches in RIGHT SECTION. Battalion spread out as follows. 3 Platoons of D Coy in Trenches D.19.+20 C Company in KNARESBORO' CASTLE, THE PUMP ROOM, CLIFFORD'S TOWER, and the WILLOWS. A Company and 1 Platoon of D Coy at H.Q. Near LA BELLE ALLIANCE. B Coy on CANAL BANK (E). Front line Trenches in poor condition.	Knight Capt.
Trenches D.19 +20	24th		Heavy Frost. Quiet day - Trenches in very bad condition	Knight Capt.
- -	25th		Heavy Frost and mist all day - little work could be done owing to state of ground. Quiet day	Knight Capt.
- -	26th		Heavy Frost. Little artillery fire - Front line receiving some WHIZZ-BANGS - no damage done	Knight Capt.

Army Form C. 2118.

WAR DIARY
or
INTELLIGENCE SUMMARY.
(Erase heading not required.)

Instructions regarding War Diaries and Intelligence Summaries are contained in F. S. Regs., Part II. and the Staff Manual respectively. Title pages will be prepared in manuscript.

(24.)

Place	Date	Hour	Summary of Events and Information	Remarks and references to Appendices
Trenches D.19-D.20.	Nov. 27th		Heavy Frost. Vicinity of Wilson's Farm and La Brique shelled - nothing further. Happened during the day. Relieved in the trenches by the 1/6th Bn West Yorkshire Regt.	Smyth Capt
In Div. reserve Coppernollhoek Camp No 2.	28th		The Battalion in Divisional Reserve. Heavy frost. Little work owing to lack of material	Smyth Capt
—	29th		Rain. No material arrived. Working party of 2 officers +100 other ranks.	Smyth Capt
—	30th		Working party of 2 officers +100 other ranks. Rain at intervals during day - State of Camp very bad	Smyth Capt

146th Inf.Bde.
49th Div.

1/7th BATTN. THE WEST YORKSHIRE REGIMENT.

D E C E M B E R

1 9 1 5

WAR DIARY
INTELLIGENCE SUMMARY.
(Erase heading not required.)

Army Form C. 2118.

Place	Date	Hour	Summary of Events and Information	Remarks and references to Appendices
Coppernollshock Camp No 2	Dec 1st		Work in Camp progressing. Tram lines laid and Huts completed as far as material permits. Working party 2 officers 100 other ranks	Knight Capt.
	2nd		Nothing special to report. Working party 2 officers 100 other ranks	Knight Capt.
	3rd		Wet. Camp grids made and laid in various parts of Camp. Material for more huts arrived. Working party 2 officers + 100 other ranks.	Knight Capt.
	4th		Wet and very windy. Working party of 2 officers + 100 other ranks.	Knight Capt.
	5th		Relieved 1/6th West Yorkshire Regt as Right Support Battalion. Battalion disposed as follows :- 'A' Coy Canal Bank. 'B' Coy Hale's Farm. C+'D' Coys HQ at Elverdinghe Chateau. 'B' Company has suffered whilst detrussing at Dawson's Corner 1 man slightly wounded.	Knight Capt.
	6th		Nothing special to report.	Knight Capt.
	7th		Relieved 1/6th West Yorkshire Regt as Left Front Battalion. Trenches in very bad condition	Knight Capt.

Army Form C. 2118.

26.

WAR DIARY
or
INTELLIGENCE SUMMARY.
(Erase heading not required.)

Instructions regarding War Diaries and Intelligence Summaries are contained in F. S. Regs., Part II. and the Staff Manual respectively. Title pages will be prepared in manuscript.

Place	Date	Hour	Summary of Events and Information	Remarks and references to Appendices
Trenches	Dec			
D.21, D.22	8th	AM 5	Bombardment of Enemy front line between ESSEN FARM and KRUPP FARM, communication trenches and roads & his Second line.	
		5:30	Bombardment ceased.	
		5:30-6:30	Bombardment taken up by M.G.	
		11-12	Enemy retaliated on our front line, Support line - Canal Bank and roads leading to Canal. Damage considerable in places but slight on the whole, considering the intensity of the bombardment. Our casualties were 5 killed and 13 wounded, now very slightly. Parapet in lots D.21 & D.22 damaged. No casualties on of the front line. The Trenches on our right and left were damaged in places. The 1/6th Bn WEST YORKSHIRE REGT on our right having suffered several casualties.	EngyApp
	9th	AM 5-6	Bombardment of Canal Bank and approaches - no damage done. Bridgehead on Bridge 4 had some named escape. Rain all day.	EngyApp
	10th	PM 6-10	Slight Artillery bombardment throughout day. Enemy dropped a considerable number of shells about ESSEX FARM and BRIDGE A. Same near but Rained most of the day.	EngyApp
	11th		A Quiet day. Rained most of the day. Relieved in trenches by 1/8th Bn WEST YORKSHIRE REGT - the Battalion becomes RIGHT SUPPORT.	EngyApp

Army Form C. 2118.

WAR DIARY
or
INTELLIGENCE SUMMARY.
(Erase heading not required.)

(27)

Instructions regarding War Diaries and Intelligence Summaries are contained in F. S. Regs., Part II. and the Staff Manual respectively. Title pages will be prepared in manuscript.

Place	Date	Hour	Summary of Events and Information	Remarks and references to Appendices
RIGHT SUPPORT	DEC^R 12TH		Nothing to report. HALES FARM shelled - no damage done.	Angst/Capt.
" "	13TH		Relieved the 1/6TH B^N WEST YORKSHIRE REG^T on our left in Trenches D.19. 20. Trenches in very bad condition. 1/5TH B^T WEST YORKSHIRE REG^T on our left in D.21 and D.22. and XIV Division on our right.	Angst/Capt.
Trenches D.19 . 20	14TH		A quiet day. Aeroplanes on both sides very active.	Angst/Capt.
" "	15TH		Slight bombardment of front line and communication trenches - no damage done. Wet day. 1/6TH B^N WEST YORKSHIRE REG^T replaced 1/5TH B^T WEST YORKSHIRE REG^T on our left.	Angst/Capt.
" "	16TH	3-4 PM	Bombardment of the X line from ZOUAVE VILLA to IRISH FARM no damage done.	Angst/Capt.
" "	17TH	10.30 AM 12.10 PM 12.15 2.30	Intense Bombardment of line FOCH FARM - LA BELLE ALLIANCE - IRISH FARM) Shells of all sizes. Bombardment ceased. - No damage done. Our Artillery bombarded Enemy front line opposite E.27 - F.30. Enemy replying all along the line - very scattered.	Angst/Capt.
		7.20	Relieved in Trenches by 1/5TH B^T WEST YORKSHIRE REG^T the Battalion becoming RIGHT SUPPORT	Angst/Capt.
RIGHT SUPPORT	18TH		Nothing to report.	Angst/Capt.

1577 Wt.W10791/1773 500,000 1/15 D.D. & L. A.D.S.S./Forms/C. 2118.

Army Form C. 2118.

WAR DIARY
or
INTELLIGENCE SUMMARY.
(Erase heading not required.)

Instructions regarding War Diaries and Intelligence Summaries are contained in F.S. Regs., Part II. and the Staff Manual respectively. Title pages will be prepared in manuscript.

(28).

Place	Date	Hour	Summary of Events and Information	Remarks and references to Appendices
RIGHT SUPPORT	Dec 19th	AM 5.30	Enemy attacked whole front of VIth Corps with gas - preceded by 20 minutes rapid rifle fire. Our guns opened at once and attack failed everywhere. Wind N.E. light favourable.	
		6.40	Received message to move up to Canal Bank (W) S of Bridge 4.	
		7.15	Started for above destination - morning light - ground mist fairly heavy.	
		8.30	Arrived in required position - without a shell being fired at road used by us - inspite of 2 Observation Balloons and 4 Aeroplanes, all hostile, being up at the time. The ground mist was probably too thick for observation. Formation used, En route, platoons at 100 yds. Bombardment by enemy of every registered position throughout advance, except the road used by us. The Battalion remained on W Bank of Canal, during which time the Bombardment continued to be intense. All approaches to front line being heavily shelled. The 2/Sherwood Foresters and ?BN Y&L Regt arrived after us, and were shelled, the ground must have lifted, these Regiments went to their appointed positions. The Bombardment continued throughout the entire day. All types of Shells being used including gas shells. No further attempts to come over made by enemy. Battalion remained on W BANK of Canal until going forward to relieve 1/6th BN West Yorkshire Regt in the ordinary course of events in Trenches D.21. D.22.	[signature] Capt.
Trenches D.21 D.22	20th	AM 12.45	Relief complete. Bombardment of Canal Bank continued throughout day - nothing of importance happened in front line.	
		PM 11	Bombardment of Canal Bank slackened, and finally ceased at midnight. Wind changed to Westerly during day. Damage done very slight. Casualties in Battalion very small considering intensity of Bombardment.	[signature] Capt.

1577 Wt. W10791/1773 500,000 1/15 D. D. & L. A.D.S.S./Forms/C. 2118.

Army Form C. 2118.

WAR DIARY
or
INTELLIGENCE SUMMARY.
(Erase heading not required.)

Instructions regarding War Diaries and Intelligence Summaries are contained in F. S. Regs., Part II. and the Staff Manual respectively. Title pages will be prepared in manuscript.

(29)

Place	Date	Hour	Summary of Events and Information	Remarks and references to Appendices
TRENCHES D.21. D.22	Dec.R. 21st		Bridges on Canal Bank shelled at odd times during day – No damage done. Occasional bursts of Artillery on roads leading to all bridges.	Kingdy Capt
-,,-	22nd		Comparatively quiet day – nothing to report.	Kingdy Capt
-,,-	23rd		Quiet day (5 officers from 2nd R.B. attached to our line – (XXIVth Divn)) Relieved in the Trenches by 1/8th Bn West Yorkshire Regt.	Kingdy Capt
RIGHT SUPPORT	24th		Dispositions – HQ & 2 Coys. (Arty) at Elverdinghe – 2 Coys. (C&D) W bank of Canal S of Bridge 4. Nothing to report. Quiet day	Kingdy Capt
-,,-	25th		Quiet day. Relieved the 1/5th Bn West Yorkshire Regt. in Trenches D 19 & 20	Kingdy Capt
TRENCHES D 19 & 20	26th		La Belle Alliance shelled on and off throughout day. Canal Bridges shelled – no damage done	Kingdy Capt
-,,-	27th		Heavy bombardment of area – no damage done. Wind changed to dangerous quarter, extra precautions against gas attack taken.	Kingdy Capt
-,,-	28th		Area again shelled - especially La Belle Alliance - great percentage of 'DUDS' - no damage done.	Kingdy Capt
-,,-	29th		Quiet day on the whole. La Belle Alliance being the only place in area btn shelled. Relieved in Trenches by the 10th Bn Durham Light Infantry (XIVth Divn) Battalion on relief moved to CAMP C. (Sqr L. 3 Sheet 27)	Kingdy Capt

Army Form C. 2118.

WAR DIARY
~~INTELLIGENCE SUMMARY.~~
(Erase heading not required.)

Instructions regarding War Diaries and Intelligence Summaries are contained in F. S. Regs., Part II. and the Staff Manual respectively. Title pages will be prepared in manuscript.

(30)

Place	Date 1915	Hour	Summary of Events and Information	Remarks and references to Appendices
CAMP C. (Ref: L.3. Sheet 27)	Dec^R 30TH	2.30 P.M.	Battalion moved by march route to HOUTKERQUE — into billets.	Army Corps
HOUTKERQUE	31ST	2.30 P.M.	Battalion moved by march route to WORMHOUDT — into rest billets.	Army Corps

1-1-16

C.W. Netley Lieut Col.
Cmd^g 1/7th Bⁿ WEST YORKSHIRE REG^T.

146/49

1/7th W. Yorks. Regt.

Jan

Vol X

49

Army Form C. 2118.

WAR DIARY
or
INTELLIGENCE SUMMARY.
(Erase heading not required.)

Instructions regarding War Diaries and Intelligence Summaries are contained in F. S. Regs., Part II. and the Staff Manual respectively. Title pages will be prepared in manuscript.

Place	Date 1916	Hour	Summary of Events and Information	Remarks and references to Appendices
WORMHOUDT	JAN. 1st		Battalion in billets in the vicinity of the town - mostly to the North.	Knight Capt
"	2nd		Nothing to report. Baggage brought up from old Transport lines.	Knight Capt
"	3rd		Transport horses inspected. 29 put on sick lines.	Knight Capt
"	4th		Companies fitting new clothes etc.	Knight Capt
"	5th		New Programme of Work for Rest Period commenced.	Knight Capt
"	6th		Brigade Route March. Warm Commander 2nd Army who presented 2 DCM's + MM to the Battalion (A/c Cowgill + A/c Inglety)	Knight Capt
"	7th		Nothing to report	Knight Capt
"	8th		Nothing to report	Knight Capt
"	9th		Nothing to report	Knight Capt
"	10th		Nothing to report	Knight Capt
"	11th		Nothing to report	Knight Capt
"	12th		Nothing to report	Knight Capt

Army Form C. 2118.

WAR DIARY
or
INTELLIGENCE SUMMARY.
(Erase heading not required.)

Instructions regarding War Diaries and Intelligence Summaries are contained in F. S. Regs., Part II. and the Staff Manual respectively. Title pages will be prepared in manuscript.

Place	Date 1916	Hour	Summary of Events and Information	Remarks and references to Appendices
MORNYHOUDT	13th Jan		Nothing to report	Knyff Capt.
-	14th		Nothing to report	Knyff Capt.
-	15th		Brigade moved by march route to vicinity of BOLLEZEELE, MERCKEGHEM & MILLAM	Knyff Capt.
MERCKEGHEM	16th		Brigade moved by march route to vicinity of ZUTKERQUE	Knyff Capt.
ZUTKERQUE	17th		Brigade moved by march route to CALAIS, Camp 6, on the CHAMP DE L'ALMA	Knyff Capt.
CALAIS	18th		Nothing to report	Knyff Capt.
-	19th		Programme of training continued	Knyff Capt.
-	20th		Nothing to report.	Knyff Capt.
-	21st		Battalion first armed with "Lewis" machine gun.	
-	22nd		Nothing to report	
-	23rd		Brigade Machine gun company formed.	
-	24th		Nothing to report	
-	25th		Nothing to report.	
-	26th		Nothing to report	
-	27th		Inspection of Battalion by Brigadier General M.D. GORING-JONES (Comd. G.O.C. 116 Brigade)	

Army Form C. 2118.

WAR DIARY
or
INTELLIGENCE SUMMARY.
(Erase heading not required.)

Instructions regarding War Diaries and Intelligence Summaries are contained in F.S. Regs., Part II. and the Staff Manual respectively. Title pages will be prepared in manuscript.

Place	Date 1916	Hour	Summary of Events and Information	Remarks and references to Appendices
Calais	Jany 28		Nothing to report.	g.c.s. for L.M.C.H.
—	29		Parts I & II of Brigade Champion ship announced (Part I: Cleanliness Turn out.) (Part II: Signalling.) First: 1/7th West Yorkshire Regt	g.c.s. for L.M.C.H.
—	30		Nothing to report.	Strength Copy.
—	31		Nothing to report.	Strength Copy.

Albert P. Park Lieut. Col.

Comd 1/7th West Yorkshire Regt

146/+9

W.A.R. DIARY
  1/7 WEST. YORKS. REGT

          Feb 1916.
          Vol.
          XI

146/+9

Army Form C. 2118.

WAR DIARY
or
INTELLIGENCE SUMMARY.
(Erase heading not required.)

Instructions regarding War Diaries and Intelligence Summaries are contained in F. S. Regs., Part II. and the Staff Manual respectively. Title pages will be prepared in manuscript.

Place	Date	Hour	Summary of Events and Information	Remarks and references to Appendices
FEBRUARY	FEB.			
CALAIS	1st	5 PM	Moved from Camp to Fontinette Station	Singer Capt.
		8	Foggy by train - destination unknown.	Singer Capt.
LONGEAU	2nd	3 AM	Arrived and marched to FOURDRINOY into billets	Singer Capt.
FOURDRINOY	3rd		In billets in village - nothing to report.	Singer Capt.
"	4th		Orders received to proceed to PICQUIGNY.	Singer Capt.
"	5th		Proceeded to PICQUIGNY into billets	Singer Capt.
PICQUIGNY	6th		Nothing to report.	Singer Capt.
"	7th		Nothing to report.	Singer Capt.
"	8th		Practice Alarm. ½ Battalion's rifles tested.	Singer Capt.
"	9th		½ Battalion's rifles tested. Orders received to move up to Fluchers E. of BOUZINCOURT	Singer Capt.
"	10th	9.30 AM	Marched to MOLLIENS-AU-BOIS. In billets for the night.	Singer Capt.
MOLLIENS-AU-BOIS	11th	9.30 PM	Left MOLLIENS-AU-BOIS for BOUZINCOURT arriving there at 1.30 p.m. In billets, very close owing to Battalions of 32nd Div. being our billet	Singer Capt.

Army Form C. 2118.

WAR DIARY
or
INTELLIGENCE SUMMARY.
(Erase heading not required.)

Instructions regarding War Diaries and Intelligence Summaries are contained in F. S. Regs., Part II. and the Staff Manual respectively. Title pages will be prepared in manuscript.

Place	Date 1916	Hour	Summary of Events and Information	Remarks and references to Appendices
BOUZINCOURT	FEBY 12TH	PM 4	Marched off by Companies into Support relieving 15TH BN LANCASHIRE FUSILIERS and 1 Company 16TH BN NORTHUMBER-LAND FUSILIERS. Battalion disposed as follows HQ and 2 Companies at AUTHUILLE, 1 Company at GORDON CASTLE in THIEPVAL WOOD, and 1 Company occupying McMAHON'S POST, and MILL KEEP. The Company at GORDON CASTLE coming under the Command of O.C. 1/8TH BN WEST YORKSHIRE REGT for tactical purposes. (Left Battalion) Transport and Stores remain at BOUZINCOURT.	Sngd Capt. Sngd Capt.
IN SUPPORT AUTHUILLE	13TH		A few shots fell in village during afternoon - no damage done. McMAHON'S POST and MILL KEEP handed over to 1/48TH BDE - our Company coming over to AUTHUILLE	Sngd Capt.
—	14TH	PM 10	A few shots during afternoon, one very close to HQ - no damage done. ~~Orders received to take over McMAHONS POST and MILL KEEP to 1/48TH BDE~~ Orders received to send one Company to JOHNSTON'S POST, to come under orders of O.C. 1/6TH BN WEST YORKSHIRE REGT for tactical purposes (Right Battalion).	Sngd Capt.
—	15TH		Nothing of importance to report. War. Very quiet	Sngd Capt.
—	16TH		Officers and N.C.Os went round area (wire). O Very quiet day	Sngd Capt.
—	17TH	AM	Officers and N.C.Os went round our line. Very quiet.	Sngd Capt.
—	18TH	3.0	Bombardment some way N of our line.	Sngd Capt.

WAR DIARY
or
INTELLIGENCE SUMMARY.

Army Form C. 2118.

Place	Date 1916 FEBY	Hour	Summary of Events and Information	Remarks and references to Appendices
AUTHUILLE (In Support)	19th		Bombardment on Right of Brigade immediately on our left (108th) Nothing happened.	Knight Capt
AUTHUILLE (In Support)	20th		Relieved 1/8th Bn West Yorkshire Regt in G.R. Section of Trenches (1/5th West Yorkshire Regt on our Right — 9th Royal Irish Fusiliers (108th Bde) on our Left) Relief completed without incident	Knight Capt
In Trenches G 2	21st		A quiet day with the exception of a few Trench mortars which did no damage	Knight Capt.
"	22nd		Nothing of importance happened. Some Rifle Shots and Trench mortars during day. The enemy sent some Very Lights and some shells.	Knight Capt.
"	23rd		A portion of "C" Company's line was shelled with Whizz Bangs - Killing 2 and wounding 2 - Includg in which are the Right Germans sent on gas. No material damage done. Very cold and showery	Knight Capt.
"	24th	PM 11	Nothing of importance happened. Supped during morning. Relieved by 1/6th West Yorkshire Regt Blake. Owing to inclement weather, the Battalion was in trenches relieving for 4 days	Knight Capt.
MARTINSART	25th	AM 3	The Battalion arrived in Billets in Brigade Reserve.	Knight Capt.

Army Form C. 2118.

WAR DIARY
or
INTELLIGENCE SUMMARY.
(Erase heading not required.)

Instructions regarding War Diaries and Intelligence Summaries are contained in F. S. Regs., Part II. and the Staff Manual respectively. Title pages will be prepared in manuscript.

Place	Date 1916	Hour	Summary of Events and Information	Remarks and references to Appendices
MARTINSART	FEBY 26th		Nothing of importance happened. 1 Officer and 150 on fatigue.	App 7 Capt
"	27th		Nothing of importance happened. 1 Officer and 150 on fatigue and digging parties	App 7 Capt
"	28th		Nothing of importance happened. 1 Officer and 150 on fatigue and digging parties	App 7 Capt
"	29th		Nothing of importance happened during the day. A heavy bombardment took place some distance to the South during the evening.	
		6 PM	Started from MARTINSART to relieve 1/8th Bn. WEST YORKSHIRE REGT in trenches in G.2. Section.	
		10.40	Relief Complete.	

C H Pettey Major
Commanding 1/7th Bn West Yorkshire Regt.

1/7 W York Regt

Vol XII

March 1916.

Army Form C. 2118.

WAR DIARY
or
INTELLIGENCE SUMMARY.
(Erase heading not required.)

Place	Date 1916	Hour	Summary of Events and Information	Remarks and references to Appendices
In Trenches G.2 Section	March 1st		Took up line as before 1/5th Bn WEST YORKSHIRE REGT on our RIGHT and 9TH BN ROYAL IRISH FUSILIERS (ULSTER DIVISION) on our left.	Kingsly Capt.
"	2nd		Nothing to report	Kingsly Capt.
"	3rd		Snowed all day. Nothing to report. Orders received that 36th Divn would relieve 49th Divn on line.	Kingsly Capt.
"	4th		Snowed during day. Situation very quiet nothing to report. Officers from 9th ROYAL INNISKILLING FUSILIERS visited line previous to taking over. Orders received that 109th Bde would relieve 146th Bde on night 4/5 – 5/6th	Kingsly Capt.
"	5th		Relieved in the Trenches by 9th Bn ROYAL INNISKILLING FUSILIERS. After relief Battalion proceeded to BOUZINCOURT.	Kingsly Capt.
BOUZINCOURT	6th	A.M.	Battalion in Billets. Pincers & draft of 155 men and 1 officer.	Kingsly Capt.
		3 PM	Started on march to HARPONVILLE	Kingsly Capt.
HARPONVILLE	7th		Battalion in Billets. In CORPS RESERVE. Nothing to report.	Kingsly Capt.
"	8th		Working party 2 Officers & 250 Other ranks for road making.	Kingsly Capt.

Army Form C. 2118.

WAR DIARY
or
INTELLIGENCE SUMMARY.
(Erase heading not required.)

Instructions regarding War Diaries and Intelligence Summaries are contained in F.S. Regs., Part II. and the Staff Manual respectively. Title pages will be prepared in manuscript.

Place	Date 1916	Hour	Summary of Events and Information	Remarks and references to Appendices
	March			
HARPONVILLE	9th		1 officer and 125 other ranks for road making.	Sgt/Capt.
—	10th		Same fatigue as above. Nothing to report.	Sgt/Capt.
—	11th		Fatigues as above. Orders received to move to CONTAI and FRECHENCOURT for work on FRECHENCOURT–DAOURS light railway.	Sgt/Capt.
—	12th		B & D Companies to CONTAI. A & C Companies to FRECHENCOURT. H.Q., Bombers, Transport and Stores remain at HARPONVILLE.	Sgt/Capt.
—	13th		Fatigues of 250 from both CONTAI and FRECHENCOURT.	Sgt/Capt.
—	14th		H.Q., Bombers, Transport and Stores move to FRECHENCOURT. Usual fatigues on light railway.	Sgt/Capt.
FRECHENCOURT	15th		Fatigues on light railway. 19th Bn. MANCHESTER Regt. arrived in FRECHENCOURT. B & D Companies moved up to work to FRECHENCOURT and BÉHENCOURT respectively.	Sgt/Capt.
—	16th		Fatigues on light railway. 500 men.	Sgt/Capt.
—	17th		Same fatigues as above. Draft of 2 officers and 30 o.r.	Sgt/Capt.
—	18th		Usual fatigues.	Sgt/Capt.
—	19th		Usual fatigues.	Sgt/Capt.

Army Form C. 2118.

WAR DIARY
or
INTELLIGENCE SUMMARY.
(Erase heading not required.)

Instructions regarding War Diaries and Intelligence Summaries are contained in F. S. Regs., Part II. and the Staff Manual respectively. Title pages will be prepared in manuscript.

Place	Date	Hour	Summary of Events and Information	Remarks and references to Appendices
FRÉCHENCOURT	MARCH 20th		Draft of 1 Officer and 45 o.r. arrive. Usual fatigues on railway	Sgt. Capt.
"	21st		Usual fatigues on railway. Nothing to report	Sgt. Capt.
"	22nd		Usual fatigues on railway.	Sgt. Capt.
"	23rd		Same daily fatigues on railway.	Sgt. Capt.
"	24th		Same daily fatigues on railway.	Sgt. Capt.
"	25th		Half day on railway fatigue. Work practically complete.	Sgt. Capt.
"	26th		No further working parties required from the Battalion.	Sgt. Capt.
"	27th		Drills for new Drafts - Classes for Specialists.	Sgt. Capt.
"	28th		Drills for new Drafts. Classes for Specialists.	Sgt. Capt.
"	29th		19th Bn. Manchester Regt. left the village and were replaced by 18th Bn. Manchester Regt.	Sgt. Capt.
"	30th		Drills for new Drafts and usual classes. Battalion inspected by F.M. Earl Kitchener of Khartoum K.G. K.P. etc on Béhencourt Road.	Sgt. Capt.

Army Form C. 2118.

WAR DIARY
or
INTELLIGENCE SUMMARY.

(Erase heading not required.)

Instructions regarding War Diaries and Intelligence Summaries are contained in F. S. Regs., Part II. and the Staff Manual respectively. Title pages will be prepared in manuscript.

Place	Date	Hour	Summary of Events and Information	Remarks and references to Appendices
FRECHENCOURT	March 31st		Drills for New Drafts. Specialists. Remainder of Companies at disposal of Company Commanders for Training. Issue of Summer drawers.	Sgt Capt.

Albert S Neil
Lieut. Col.
Cmdg 1/7th West Yorkshire Regt.

146/49

1/7 W York Regt

Vol XIII

April 1916

WAR DIARY
or
INTELLIGENCE SUMMARY.
(Erase heading not required.)

Army Form C. 2118.

Place	Date APRIL	Hour	Summary of Events and Information	Remarks and references to Appendices
FREQUENCOURT	1st		Company Training. Recruits Drills and Specialist classes	Regtl Capt
	2nd		Nothing to report	Regtl Capt
	3rd		Company Training. Recruits Drills and Specialist classes	Regtl Capt
	4th		" " " " "	Regtl Capt
	5th		" " " " "	Regtl Capt
	6th		" " " " "	Regtl Capt
	7th	10 AM	Received orders to move to Vignacourt	Regtl Capt
	8th	8.15 AM	Field day with Divison. Advance at 2 pm was in bivouac by 5 pm. The whole of the 146th Bde in Vignacourt.	Regtl Capt
VIGNACOURT	9th		Divine Service	Regtl Capt
	10th		Coming out on Stables. Bn on duty	Regtl Capt
	11th		Continued training of men to the value for Rotate digging, owing to cultivation.	Regtl Capt

1577 Wt. W10791/1773 500,000 1/15 D. D. & L. A.D.S.S./Forms/C. 2118.

Army Form C. 2118.

WAR DIARY
or
INTELLIGENCE SUMMARY.
(Erase heading not required.)

Place	Date April	Hour	Summary of Events and Information	Remarks and references to Appendices
VIGNACOURT	12th		New Programme of Company Training adopted. A very wet day	Asst Capt.
—	13th		Training continued. Wet day	Asst Capt.
—	14th		Training continued. Nothing to report	Asst Capt.
—	15th		Training continued. The Battalion completed its first year's Active Service	Asst Capt.
—	16th		Divine Service	Asst Capt.
—	17th		Company Training. Commanding Officer and 2 Officers per Company for Tactical Scheme at NAOURS. Very wet.	Asst Capt.
—	18th		Training in Billets. Too wet to go out	Asst Capt.
—	19th		Training in Billets. Too wet to go out	Asst Capt.
—	20th		Training except in Parade outside. Ground very heavy	Asst Capt.
—	21st		Rained all day	Asst Capt.
—	22nd		Scheme at NAOURS postponed owing to rain	Asst Capt.

Army Form C. 2118.

WAR DIARY
or
INTELLIGENCE SUMMARY.
(Erase heading not required.)

Instructions regarding War Diaries and Intelligence Summaries are contained in F. S. Regs., Part II. and the Staff Manual respectively. Title pages will be prepared in manuscript.

Place	Date APRIL	Hour	Summary of Events and Information	Remarks and references to Appendices
VIGNACOURT	23rd		Divine Service. Combined parade of 7th and 8th Battalions. Fine day.	Sgd Capt.
—	24th		Scheme at NAOURS carried out. Hot and fine.	Sgd Capt.
—	25th	2.30	Battalion marched out to FLIXECOURT. 2 Companies to VILLE - LE - MARCLET. Very hot marching.	Sgd Capt.
FLIXECOURT	26th		2 Companies attached to IVth Army Infantry School of Instruction. Remainder training coys as for ville. Fine and very hot.	Sgd Capt.
—	27th		Training coys as for parade. Fatigues etc for School. Fine and very hot.	Sgd Capt.
—	28th		Training. Very hot.	Sgd Capt.
—	29th		Nothing to report.	Sgd Capt.
—	30th		Divine Service.	Sgd Capt.

W D Ottley Major
Cmdg 1/7 West Yorkshire Regt.

Army Form C. 2118.

1/7 West York Infantry Reg.

146/49

WAR DIARY
or
INTELLIGENCE SUMMARY

(Erase heading not required.)

Place	Date	Hour	Summary of Events and Information	Remarks and references to Appendices
FLIXECOURT	1916 MAY 1st		Nothing to report. Training. Attack practice	Sgt Capt.
— . —	2nd		Nothing to report. Rain stopped training.	O.C.H. Yt.
— . —	3rd		Fine. Tactical exercise for C.O., adjutant & company commanders at Brigade.	O.C.H. Yt.
— . —	4th		Nothing to report. Training. Bayonet fighting.	O.C.H. Yt.
— . —	5th		Training. Attack practice, musketry. Tactical exercise for C.O., Adjutant & Company Commanders at Brigade	O.C.H. Yt.
— . —	6th		Training. Musketry.	O.C.H. Yt.
— . —	7th		Nothing to report. Church parade cancelled owing to rain.	O.C.H. Yt.
— . —	8th		Nothing to report. Training. Musketry.	O.C.H. Yt.
— . —	9th		Nothing to report. Training. Route march. Bayonet fighting.	O.C.H. Yt.
— . —	10th		Training. Musketry.	O.C.H. Yt.

Army Form C. 2118.

WAR DIARY
or
INTELLIGENCE SUMMARY
(Erase heading not required.)

1/1 West Yorkshire Regt.

Place	Date 1916 MAY	Hour	Summary of Events and Information	Remarks and references to Appendices
FLIXECOURT	11th		Training. Bayonet fighting. Judging distance. Extended Order drill	C.X.F.F.H.
FLIXECOURT	12th		Training. Practice attack.	C.X.F.F.H.
—	13th		Training. Bayonet fighting. Kit Inspection	C.X.F.F.H.
—	14th		Tactical scheme for Battalion scouts. Divine service followed by a celebration of Holy Communion.	C.X.F.H.
—	15th		Nothing to report. Training. Extended Order Drill, Bayonet fighting.	C.X.F.H.
—	16th		Training. Practice attack	C.X.F.H.
—	17th		Training. Musketry.	C.X.F.F.H.
—	18th		Training. Musketry, Close Order Drill. Bayonet fighting.	H.F.F.H.
—	19th		Training. School Fatigues	Con.
—	20th		Training. Demonstration at Army School	Con.
—	21st		Nothing to report. Church Parade followed by Holy Communion. Co. Adjutant & Officers at VIGNACOURT for tactical exercise.	Con.
—	22nd		Nothing to report. Company Training. Musketry. Bayonet fighting. Outposts	Con.
—	23rd		Battalion moved to Hogencourt VIGNACOURT	Con. ord.
VIGNACOURT	24th		Brigade Day - Outposts	Con. ord.
—	2.5th		Attack on trenches by the Battalion	Con.

Army Form C. 2118.

1/1 West Yorkshire Regt

Vol 14

WAR DIARY
or
INTELLIGENCE SUMMARY
(Erase heading not required.)

Place	Date	Hour	Summary of Events and Information	Remarks and references to Appendices
VIGNACOURT	1916 MAY 26		Battalion - Billets in VIGNACOURT FOREST	
"	27		Brigade - Church Service S.W. of OVEN Church Parade	
"	28		Battalion moved by march to TOUTENCOURT	
On March	29		do. to AVELUY WOOD	
"	30			
"	31		Battalion digging under instructions of the 36th Division	

Albert Smith
Lt Colonel
Commanding 1/1 West Yorks

146th Brigade.

49th Division.

1/7th BATTALION

WEST YORKSHIRE REGIMENT

JUNE 1916

Army Form C. 2118.

WAR DIARY
or
INTELLIGENCE SUMMARY
(Erase heading not required.)

1/7 West Yorkshire Regiment Pt 15

Place	Date	Hour	Summary of Events and Information	Remarks and references to Appendices
AVELUY WOOD	1		Nothing to report – Battalion digging Trench under R.E. 36th Division	
	2		3 A.M. Heavy 1/2 Hour 5 minute bombardment of AVELUY WOOD – No casualties. Digging under 36th Div R.E.	
	3		Nothing to report – Night digging on 36 Div. R.E.	
	4		Volunteers Chinese Practice – Night digging under 36 & Div. R.E.	
	5		Nothing to report. Night drilling under 36 & Div. R.E.	
	6		Nothing to report	
	7		do —	
	8		do —	
	9		do	
	10		do	
	11		do	
	12		do	
	13		do	
	14		do	
	15		do	
	16		do	
	17		do	
	18		do	
	19		Battn. moved to HEDAUVILLE WOOD	
HEDAUVILLE WOOD	20		Nothing to report – Digging at D.A.S	
	21		do	
	22		Battn. moved to PUCHEVILLERS	
PUCHEVILLERS	23		Nothing to report – refitting	
	24		do	
	25			

Army Form C. 2118.

WAR DIARY
or
INTELLIGENCE SUMMARY

(Erase heading not required.)

1/5 East Yorkshire Regt

Place	Date	Hour	Summary of Events and Information	Remarks and references to Appendices
PUCHEVILLERS	26		Nothing to report	less
—	27		Battalion moved to VARENNES	CMS
VARENNES	28		Nothing to report	Cns
do	29		do	Cns
do	30		Battalion moved to Assembly Trenches in AVELUY WOOD	Cns

Hurtshill
Lt Colonel
Commanding 1/5 East Yorkshire Regt.

146th Inf.Bde.
49th Div.

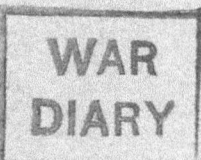

1/7th BATTN. THE WEST YORKSHIRE REGIMENT.

J U L Y

1 9 1 6

WAR DIARY or **INTELLIGENCE SUMMARY**

Army Form C. 2118.

1/46 9 7 West Yorkshire Regiment

Place	Date	Hour	Summary of Events and Information	Remarks and references to Appendices
AVELUY WOOD	July 1	9 A.M.	Orders were received for the Battalion to move to Assembly trenches in THIEPVAL WOOD – This movement was completed by 12 noon without loss.	
THIEPVAL WOOD		3.30 P.M.	The 146 Infantry Brigade ordered an attack on THIEPVAL VILLAGE by the 5th & 6th Battn. W. York Regt. whilst 8th Battn. in support and the 7th Battn. in reserve. — The 7th Battn. then moved into Assembly Trenches in the vicinity of BELFAST CITY in THIEPVAL WOOD but was immediately ordered to reinforce the original British front line. On completion of this move C & D Companies were ordered to reinforce the Captured German "A" line but retired from these lines under orders received from the 36th Division during the night 1/2 July 1916.	O/B
THIEPVAL WOOD	2	—	A & B Companies were gradually withdrawn from the front line trenches in the wood and assembled in trenches near to GORDON CASTLE — C & D Companies remaining in the front line. Orders were issued that the 146th Infantry Brigade would be relieved by the 147 & 148 Infantry Brigades.	Cas. Cas.
AVELUY WOOD		3.15 P.M.	The relief being completed — The Battn. reported "all in hand" Casualties in Assembly Trenches AVELUY WOOD.	Cas. Cas.
— do —	3	11 P.M.	Battn. moved to hutments in MARTINSART WOOD	Cas.
MARTINSART WOOD	4	—	Nothing to report	Cas.
— do —	5	—	do	Cas.
— do —	6	—	do 2 Officers + 100 men detailed as Burying party in THIEPVAL WOOD	Cas.
— do —	7	11 P.M.	MOVED to AVELUY WOOD.	Cas.
AVELUY WOOD	8	3 A.M.	Batt. relieved 8 L.N. LANCS in LEIPSIC SALIENT	Cas.
LEIPSIC SALIENT	9	8 P.M.	Batt. relieved by 1/6 W. YORK R.gt — Moved to S. BLUFF AUTHVILLE. Carrying parties to front line, all night	Cas.
S. BLUFF AUTHUILLE	10		Nothing to report — Carrying parties to front line.	Cas.
— do —	11		do	Cas.
— do —	12		Relieved 1/6 W. YORK R.gt in LEIPSIC SALIENT — Night of 12/13th Bosch launching attack on left regiment.	Cas.
LEIPSIC SALIENT	13		Nothing to report	Cas.

Army Form C. 2118.

WAR DIARY
or
INTELLIGENCE SUMMARY

1/7 West Yorkshire Regiment

(Erase heading not required.)

Place	Date 1916	Hour	Summary of Events and Information	Remarks and references to Appendices
LEIPSIG SALIENT	July 14	2.15 AM	Battn. attack (2 Companies only committed) on German line on our left - There was not successful - immediate counter attack by enemy repulsed. Relieved by 1/6th West York. Regt. & moved to S. BLUFF AUTHUILLE.	CMS
S. BLUFF AUTHUILLE	15		Nothing to report. - Carrying parties to front line.	CMS
- do -	16	8 AM	Relieved 1/5 Bn. West York Regt. in trenches in old British front line in front of AUTHUILLE (CAMPBELL POST)	CMS
		4 pm	Relief complete.	CMS
CAMPBELL POST	17		Nothing to report	CMS
"	18		do	CMS
"	19		do	CMS
"	20		do	CMS
"	21		Battn. relieved by 1/5 K.O.Y.L.I. and proceeded to MARTINSART WOOD	CMS
MARTINSART WOOD	22		Nothing to report. 2 Companies digging trench in NO MANS LAND - 2 Coys carrying	CMS
"	23		do	CMS
"	24		Battn. (less 'A' Coy) moved to FORCEVILLE - 'A' Coy moved to S. BLUFF AUTHUILLE.	CMS
FORCEVILLE	25		Nothing to report. Training & reorganisation	CMS
do	26		do	CMS
do	27		do D. Coy. relieved A. Coy at S. BLUFF.	CMS
do	28		do	CMS
do	29		do	CMS
do	30		do B. Coy relieved D. Coy at S. BLUFF	CMS
do	31		do	CMS

Hurt.Lieut
J.E.Colvil
Commanding 1/7 W.Y.R.

146th Brigade
49th Division

1/7th BATTALION

WEST YORKSHIRE REGIMENT

AUGUST 1 9 1 6

WAR DIARY
or
INTELLIGENCE SUMMARY.

(Erase heading not required.)

Army Form C. 2118.

1/7 West Yorkshire Regt.

Vol 17

Place	Date 1916 August	Hour	Summary of Events and Information	Remarks and references to Appendices
FORCEVILLE	1		Nothing to report — Training	Cas
do	2		do	Cas
do	3		Battalion relieved 1/5 Yrk. in LEIPSIC SALIENT	Cas
LEIPSIC SALT.	4		Nothing to report	Cas
do	5		do	Cas
do	6		do	Cas
do	7		Batten relieved by 1/5 W. York Rgt. proceeded to S. BLUFF less 3 coys. D Coy. Rock St. C. Coy. MERSEY St. B South Bluff.	Cas
S. BLUFF	8		A Coy to DBAN Av.	Cas
AUTHUILE	9		Nothing to report	Cas
do	10		do	Cas
LEIPSIC SALIENT	11		Battalion relieved 1/5 W. YORK Rgt in LEIPSIC Salient	Cas
do	12		Nothing to report	Cas
do	13		do relieved by 1/5 W. York Rgt. HQ and D Coy moved to S. BLUFF AUTHUILLE less A to DBAN Av. B Rodger St. C to MERSEY St.	Cas
S BLUFF	14		Nothing to report	Cas
do	15		do	Cas
do	16		do	Cas
do	17		do	Cas
do	18		Relieved by 10th Cheshire Regiment — The Battn marched to huts in ACHEUX Wood	Cas
ACHEUX WOOD	19		Kit inspection — reorganizing.	Cas

"17 West Yorkshire Rgt."

WAR DIARY
or
INTELLIGENCE SUMMARY.
(Erase heading not required.)

Army Form C. 2118.

Instructions regarding War Diaries and Intelligence Summaries are contained in F.S. Regs., Part II. and the Staff Manual respectively. Title pages will be prepared in manuscript.

Place	Date 1916 Aug	Hour	Summary of Events and Information	Remarks and references to Appendices
ACHEUX WOOD	20		Church Parade – Bathing.	Covs
do	21		Training	Covs
do	22		do	Covs
do	23		do – Lt. Col. Kerr V.D. proceeded to England	Covs
do	24		Training	Covs
do	25		do	Covs
do	26		Battn relieved 13th Cheshire Rgt. in the right sector of THIEPVAL TRENCHES (JOHNSTONE'S POST)	Covs
JOHNSTONE'S POST	27		Nothing to report	Covs
do	28		Relieved by 1/5 K.O.Y.L.I – Battn. moved to MARTINSART WOOD	Covs
MARTINSART WOOD	29		Nothing to report	Covs
do	30		do	Covs
do	31		do	Covs

CWDettey Lt. Col
Commanding 1/7th West Yorkshire Rgt.

294-
1B

146th. INFANTRY BRIGADE

49th. DIVISION

1/7th. WEST YORKSHIRE REGT.

S E P T E M B E R   1 9 1 6.

WAR DIARY
or
INTELLIGENCE SUMMARY.
(Erase heading not required.)

1/7th West Yorkshire Regt.

Army Form C. 2118.

Place	Date 1916 Sept	Hour	Summary of Events and Information	Remarks and references to Appendices
MARTINSART WOOD	1		Nothing to report	
do	2		moved to "A" Group Assembly Trenches - Aveluy Wood	
AVELUY WOOD	3	8 AM.	Moved via N. Causeway to Gordon Castle - Thiepval Wood (in reserve)	
THIEPVAL WOOD	4	4 PM.	Relieved by 148 Bde. Batn. moved to Martinsart Wood.	
MARTINSART WOOD	5		Carrying parties & working parties	
do	6		do	
do	7		The Battalion moved to Forceville less 2 Companies left as working parties in Martinsart Wood	
FORCEVILLE	8		Training	
do	9		do	
do	10		do - 2 Coys from Martinsart Wood rejoined Battn.	
do	11		do	
do	12		do	
do	13		do	
do	14		do	
do	15		do	
do	16		do	
do	17		do	
do	18		Battn. moved to Hedauville	
HEDAUVILLE	19		Training	
do	20		Relieved 1/5 KOYLI - (apx) Thiepval Sector. HQ. Johnstone's Post.	
JOHNSTONE'S POST	21		Nothing to report	
do	22		do	
do	23		do	

Army Form C. 2118.

1/7th West Yorkshire Regt.

Vol 18

WAR DIARY
or
INTELLIGENCE SUMMARY.
(Erase heading not required.)

Place	Date 1916 Sept	Hour	Summary of Events and Information	Remarks and references to Appendices
JOHNSTONE'S POST	24		Nothing to report	C/w
do	25		do	C/w
do	26		do	C/w
do	27		Relieved by 11th LANCS FUSILIERS - Battn. marched to huts in MAILLY MAILLET WOOD	C/w
MAILLY MAILLET WOOD	28		Nothing to report	C/w
do	29		Battn. marched to RAINCHEVAL	C/w
RAINCHEVAL	30		Battn. marched to HALLOY	C/w

CAP Stetty, Lt Colonel
Commanding 1/7 W York B

146/49

WAR DIARY
or
INTELLIGENCE SUMMARY.
(Erase heading not required.)

Army Form C. 2118.

1/7 West Yorkshire Regt.

Vol 19

Place	Date 1916 Oct	Hour	Summary of Events and Information	Remarks and references to Appendices
HALLOY	1		Battalion moved to COULLEMONT	CMS
COULLEMONT	2		Training - Nothing to report	CMS
do	3		do	CMS
do	4		Battalion moved to SOMARIN	CMS
SOMARIN	5		Training - Nothing to report	CMS
do	6		do	CMS
do	7		do	CMS
do	8		do	CMS
do	9		do	CMS
do	10		Battalion moved to Huttments in HUMBERCAMPS	CMS
HUMBERCAMPS	11		Training - Nothing to report	CMS
do	12		do - do -	CMS
do	13		do - do -	CMS
do	14		do - do -	CMS
do	15		do - do -	CMS
do	16		do - do -	CMS
do	17		do - do -	CMS
do	18		Battalion relieved 1/7 E. An. W. Riding Regiment in the Centre Sub Sector in front of FONQUEVILLERS 2/19	CMS
FONQUEV LERS	19		Nothing to report	CMS
do	20		do	CMS
do	21		do	CMS
do	22		do	CMS

Army Form C. 2118.

WAR DIARY
INTELLIGENCE SUMMARY.
(Erase heading not required.)

1/ West Yorkshire Regt.

Place	Date 1916 Oct.	Hour	Summary of Events and Information	Remarks and references to Appendices
FONQUEVILLERS	23		Nothing to report	Cas.
do	24		Battn. relieved by 1/8 W. York Regt. & 1 Coy 1/6 W. Riding Regt. & moved to billets in BIENVILLERS	Cas.
BIENVILLERS	25		Nothing to report — working parties	Cas.
do	26		do	Cas.
do	27		do	Cas.
do	28		do	Cas.
do	29		do	Cas.
do	30		do	Cas.
do	31		do	Cas.

W.J. Bradwurdi Major
Commanding 1/ W. York Regt.

Army Form C. 2118.

WAR DIARY
or
INTELLIGENCE SUMMARY.
(Erase heading not required.)

1/7th War Yorkshire Regt.   Vol 20

Place	Date 1916 Nov	Hour	Summary of Events and Information	Remarks and references to Appendices
BIENVILLERS	1		Nothing to report – working parties	CWS
do	2	3pm.	Relieved 1/8th Battn. W. YORK. Regt. in Right Sub-sector of Left Sector (FONQUEVILLERS)	CWS
FONQUEVILLERS	3		Nothing to report	CWS.
do	4		do	CWS
do	5		do	CWS
do	6		do	CWS
do	7		do	CWS
do	8		Relieved by 1/8th Battn. W. Yorks. Regt. — This Battn. moved to ST AMAND – Divisional Reserve	CWS
ST AMAND	9		Nothing to report – Drawing Camp	CWS
do	10		do	CWS
do	11		do	CWS
do	12		do	CWS
do	13		do	CWS
do	14		Relieved 1/8th Yorks Regt in Z Sector (Right Sub-Sector)	CWS
FONQUEVILLERS	15		Nothing to report	CWS
do	16		do	CWS
do	17		do	CWS
do	18		do	CWS
do	19		do	CWS
do	20		Relieved by 1/8th W. Yorks Regt – Battn moved into "Support" at BIENVILLERS	CWS
BIENVILLERS	21		Nothing to report – Working parties	CWS

Army Form C. 2118.

WAR DIARY
or
INTELLIGENCE SUMMARY

(Erase heading not required.)

1/7th Yorkshire Regt.

Place	Date 1916 Nov	Hour	Summary of Events and Information	Remarks and references to Appendices
BIENVILLERS	22		Nothing to report — Working Parties	CM.
do	23	6.30 AM	Battalion moved into position in HANNESCAMPS Defences — In support 1/6 h. York. Regt.	CM
		7.30 AM	Battalion returned to Billets — No Casualties.	
do	24		Nothing to report — Working Parties.	CM
do	25		do	CM
do	26	2.45 PM	Relieved 1/8th Batt. W. York Regt. in Y. Sub Sector	CM
do			Nothing to report	CM
do	28		do	CM
do	29		do	CM
do	30		do	CM

W. H. Braithwaite Major & Lt Col.
Commanding 1/7 West Yorkshire Regt.

Army Form C. 2118.

WAR DIARY
or
INTELLIGENCE SUMMARY
(Erase heading not required.)

1/7 W. York Regt.
"17 Yorkshire Regt."

Place	Date	Hour	Summary of Events and Information	Remarks and references to Appendices
FONQUEVILLERS	1916 Nov 1		Nothing to report.	
	2		Relieved by 1/8 West Yorkshire Regt. Bn. Batt. moved to SOUASTRES.	
SOUASTRE	3		Nothing to report	
	4		Battalion moved to BOUQUEMAISON	
BOUQUEMAISON	5		Nothing to report. Training	
do	6		do	
do	7		do	
do	8		do	
do	9		do	
do	10		do	
do	11		do	
do	12		do	
do	13		do	
do	14		do	
do	15		do	
do	16		do	
do	17		do	
do	18		do	
do	19		do	
do	20		do	
do	21		do	
do	22		do	
do	23		do	
do	24		do	
do	25		do	
do	26		do	
do	27		do	
do	28		do	
do	29		do	
do	30		do	

C.P. Etter
Lt. Col.
Commanding 1/7 W. Yorkshire Regt.

SECRET.

WAR DIARY.

OF

17th Batt West Yorks Regt

FOR

January 1917.

Vol 22

SECRET.

WAR DIARY.

OF

FOR 1917.

SECRET.
                    49th (West Riding) Division. No A/69/3.

D. A. G.,
    3rd Echelon,
        B A S E .

        Herewith War Diary of 1/7th Bn. West Yorks: Regt. for the month of December, forwarded in continuation of this office No. A/69/3 dated 5 : 1 : 1917.

        The delay in forwarding is regretted, but the necessary steps have been taken to ensure that the diary of this battalion is forwarded by the first of each month in future.

                                                  Major-General.

12 : 1 : 1917.   Commanding 49th (West Riding) Division.

WAR DIARY
or
INTELLIGENCE SUMMARY

(Erase heading not required.)

Army Form C. 2118.

Place	Date	Hour	Summary of Events and Information	Remarks and references to Appendices
BOUQUEMAISON	1917 May 1		Nothing to report. Training	
"	2		" " do	
"	3		" " do	
"	4		" " do	
"	5		" " do	
"	6		Battalion moved in busses to Bailleulmont.	
BAILLEULMONT C.2 Sector	7		Battalion relieved the 2nd Wiltshire Regt in C.2 Sector of the trenches.	
"	8		Battalion in trenches. C.2. Sector	
"	9		" " " "	
"	10		" " " "	
BAILLEULVAL	11		Battalion relieved in C.2 Sector by 1/8th Bn. West Yorkshire Regt. and moved to billets at Bailleulval.	
"	12		Supplying working parties	
"	13		" " "	
"	14		" " "	
C.2. Sector	15		Battalion relieved the 1/8 Bn West York Regt in C.2 Sector of the trenches.	
"	16		Battalion in trenches. C.2. Sector	
"	17		" " do	
"	18		" " do	
BAILLEUMONT	19		Battalion relieved in C.2 Sector by 1/8th Batt. West Yorkshire Regt. and moved to billets in BAILLEUMONT.	
"	20		Nothing to report. Training	
"	21		" " "	
"	22		" " "	
"	23		Battalion relieved the 1/8th Batt. West York Regt in C.2 Sector of the trenches	
C.2 Sector	24		Battalion in trenches C.2 Sector	
"	25		" " "	
"	26		" " "	
BAILLEUVAL	27		Battalion relieved in C.2 Sector by 1/8 Batt. West Yorkshire Regt. and moved to billets in BAILLEUVAL.	
"	28		Supplying working parties and training	
"	29		" " "	
"	30		" " "	
"	31		Battalion relieved the 1/8th Batt. West York Regt in C.2 Sector of the trenches	

L. H.
cmg
1/7th Batt. West York Regt.

SECRET.

WAR DIARY.

OF

1/7th Batt. West York Regt

FOR

February 1917.

Y/23

February 1917

WAR DIARY
or
INTELLIGENCE SUMMARY

Army Form C. 2118.

1/7th Bn. West Yorkshire Regt.

Place	Date	Hour	Summary of Events and Information	Remarks and references to Appendices
C 2 Sector	1		Battalion in C 2 Sector of Trenches.	
do	2		One platoon from each Company sent back to IVERGNY to make room for 4 platoons of 2/2nd London Regt to come in for instruction	
HUMBERCAMP	3		B attalion relieved in C.2 Sector by 1/8th Bn. West York. Regt. and marched to billets in HUMBERCAMP	
do	4		Nothing to report. Training and cleaning up	
do	5		do	
do	6		do	
C 2 Sector	7		Battn. relieved 1/8th W. York. Battn. in C.2 Sector	
	8		Nothing to report	
C 2th Sector	9		2/2nd London R.C. - 4 platoons replaced by 4 platoons 2/4 London Regt attached for instruction	
do	10		4 Platoons of 1/6 York. Regt. ("Valley") replaced the 4 platoons London attached away on Feby 2 rel.	
do	11		Battalion relieved by 1/8 London Regt. & moved to billets in BAILLEULMONT	
BAILLEULMONT	12		Nothing to report. Training - Bathing	
do	13		do	
do	14		do - 1/4 London Rgt. 4 platoons replaced by 2/2 London for instruction.	
do	15		do	
do			Battalion relieved 1/8 W. York Rgt. in C.2. Sector	
C.2. Sector	16		Nothing to report	
do	17		do	
do	18		do	
do	19		do 2/12 th London attached by moved to HALLOY	
do	20		do	
do	21		Battalion relieved by 2/8 London Rgt & moved to billets in BAILLEULMONT	
BAILLEULMONT	22		Battalion marched to billets at IVERGNY	
IVERGNY	23		Nothing to report	
BOUQUEMAISON	24		Battalion marched to billets at BOUQUEMAISON	
	25		do do at CROISETTE	
CROISETTE	26		do do at CAUCHY-A-LATOUR	
CAUCHY à la TOUR	27		do do at ST VENANT	
ST VENANT	28		do do at LESTREM	

C.A.Dethey Lt. Col.

Army Form C. 2118.

1/7 W York Rgt. Vol 24

WAR DIARY
or
INTELLIGENCE SUMMARY
(Erase heading not required.)

Instructions regarding War Diaries and Intelligence Summaries are contained in F.S. Regs., Part II. and the Staff Manual respectively. Title Pages will be prepared in manuscript.

Place	1917 Date Month	Hour	Summary of Events and Information	Remarks and references to Appendices
LESTREM	1		Battn. marched to LEVANTIE and relieved 1/2nd Battn. London Regt. in Brigade Reserve	
LEVANTIE	2		Nothing to report	
do	3		do	
do	4		do	
do	5		do	
do	6		do	
do	7			
FAUQUISART	8		Relieved 1/8th Bn West York Regt in the FAUQUISART or LEFT Section - Right Sub Section	
(sub section)	9		Nothing to report	
do	10		do	
do	11		do	
do	12		do	
do	13			
FAUQUISART	14		Battn. relieved by 1/8 4Bn. West Yorkshire Regt and moved into Brigade Support	
do	15		Nothing to report. Working parties	
do	16		do	
do	17		do	
do	18		do	
do	19		do	
FAUQUISART	20		Relieved 1/6th Bn West Yorkshire Regt in the FAUQUISART Section - Right Sub Section	
(Right Sub Section)	21		Nothing to report	
do	22		Enemy trench mortared right Company.	
do	23		Nothing to report	
do	24		Enemy trench mortared night and centre Coys	
do	25		Enemy trench mortared right front and rear. King inspected. All precautions taken	
do	26		Battn. relieved by 1/8th W.Y Regt and moved into Brigade Reserve	
LESTREM	27		Nothing to report	
do	28		do	
do	29		do	
do	30		do	
do	31		Relieved 1/6 Bn W.York Regt in the FAUQUISART Section - Right Sub Sect.	

E. Walling Major
Comg 1/7 th. West York Regt.

2449 Wt. W14957/M90 750,000 1/16 J.B.C. & A. Forms/C.2118/12.

Vol 25

SECRET.

WAR DIARY.

OF

4/7th Batt. West Yorks Regt

FOR

April

1917.

Army Form C. 2118.

WAR DIARY
or
INTELLIGENCE SUMMARY
(Erase heading not required.)

17th Battn. West Yorkshire Regt.

Place	Date April 1917	Hour	Summary of Events and Information	Remarks and references to Appendices
FAUQUISART Right Section	1		Nothing to report	
do	2		do	
do	3		do	
do	4		do	
do	5		1 Company of Portuguese Regts. Forces on for instruction – (34th Regt.)	
RED HOUSE	6		do	
do	7		Relieved by 1/8th Bn. West York. Regt. and moved into Brigade Support. Nothing to report	
do	8		Working parties	
do	9		do	CW3
do	10		do	CW3
do	11		do	CW3
do	12		do	
FAUQUISART Right Sub Section	13		Relieved 1/8th York Regt. in right Sub Section – FAUQUISART Sector	CW3
do	14		Nothing to report	CW3
do	15		do 1 Coy. P.E.F. attached for instruction (34th Regt.)	CW3
do	16		do	CW3
do	17		do 1 Coy. P.E.F. returned to their own formation	CW3
do	18		Relieved by 1/8 W. York Regt. – Proceeded billets in LAVENTIE – Battn. in Brigade Reserve.	CW3
LAVENTIE	19		Training	CW3
do	20		do	CW3
do	21		do	CW3
do	22		do Training for "Attack in the open"	CW3
do	23		do	CW3
do	24		Relieved 1/8th W York Regt. in Right Sub Sector – FAUQUISART Sector	CW3
Right Sub Sector FAUQUISART	25		Nothing to report	CW3
do	26		do	CW3

Army Form C. 2118.

WAR DIARY
or
INTELLIGENCE SUMMARY
(Erase heading not required.)

1/7th Batn WEST YORKSHIRE Regt.

Place	Date 1917 April	Hour	Summary of Events and Information	Remarks and references to Appendices
Right Subsector FAUQUISSART	27		1 Company 7th Regt. P.E.F. + 1 platoon 22nd Regt. Portuguese Exped. Force attached for instruction	C.W.3
do	28		Nothing to report	C.W.3
do	29		Attached Portuguese returned to their own formation	C.W.3
do	30		Nothing to report — Relieved by 1/8th Bn. W. York Rgt. — Moved to Red House as Battalion in Brigade "Support"	C.W.3

CHPetley
Lt Col.
Commanding 1/7th Bn. West Yorkshire Rgt.

Army Form C. 2118.

Vol 26
1/7th Battn. WEST YORKSHIRE REGT

WAR DIARY
or
INTELLIGENCE SUMMARY.
(Erase heading not required.)

Instructions regarding War Diaries and Intelligence Summaries are contained in F. S. Regs., Part II. and the Staff Manual respectively. Title pages will be prepared in manuscript.

Place	Date 1917 MAY	Hour	Summary of Events and Information	Remarks and references to Appendices
RED HOUSE LAVENTIE	1		Battalion in Brigade Support – Working parties – work on Forts in Rue BACQUEROT	CWB
	2		do. do.	CWB
	3		do. do.	CWB
	4		No. 1 Coy. 24th Regt. P.E.F. + 1 platoon 2 & 3rd Regt. P.E.F. attached for instruction	CWB
	5		Nothing to report – working parties.	CWB
	6		P.E.F. proceeded to billets in LAVENTIE	CWB
Regt Sub Sector FAUQUISSART	7		Relieved 1/6th W. York. Regt. in Right Sub Sector FAUQUISSART Sector of French line.	CWB
	8	9.40 pm	Nothing to report. 1/8 Battn. W. York Regt. raided German line opposite our front and took one prisoner	CWB
	9		Nothing to report	CWB
	10		do	CWB
	11		Battn. Relieved by "A" Batt. (34th Regt.) P.E.F. – Battn. moved into billets at LA GORGUE	CWB
LA GORGUE	12		Bathing etc. C. & D. Coys inoculated.	CWB
	13		Training – A & B Coy inoculated	CWB
	14		do	CWB
	15		do	CWB
	16		do	CWB
	17		Relieved 1/6th Battn. W. York Regt. at RED HOUSE in Brigade Support	CWB
RED HOUSE LAVENTIE	18		Working parties	CWB
	19			CWB

Army Form C. 2118.

WAR DIARY
or
INTELLIGENCE SUMMARY.   1/7th Battn. WEST York Regt.

(Erase heading not required.)

Instructions regarding War Diaries and Intelligence Summaries are contained in F. S. Regs., Part II. and the Staff Manual respectively. Title pages will be prepared in manuscript.

Place	Date 1917 MAY	Hour	Summary of Events and Information	Remarks and references to Appendices
RED HOUSE	20		Brigade Support - Working parties	C.W.3
LAVENTIE	21		do	C.W.3
do	22		do	C.W.3
do	23		do	C.W.3
do	24		do Relieved by 1/8th W. York Regt. & proceed to LAVENTIE - Brigade Reserve	C.W.3
LAVENTIE	25		Training	C.W.3
	26		do	C.W.3
	27		do	C.W.3
	28		do	C.W.3
	29		do	C.W.3
	30		1st Battalion relieved 1/8th Battalion W. York Regiment in the right sub sector of the FAUQUISART Sector & Dunsoir.	C.W.3
Right Sub Sector FAUQUISART Sector	31	1 A.M.	Special Coy R.E. projected gas on to the enemyline —	C.W.3

C.P. Ottley Lt. Col.
Commanding 1/7th Battalion WEST YORKSHIRE Regiment.

Vol 27

SECRET.

WAR DIARY.

OF

1/7th Batt West Yorks Regt

FOR

June 1917.

Army Form C. 2118.

WAR DIARY
or
INTELLIGENCE SUMMARY.
(Erase heading not required.)

1/7th Battalion WEST YORKSHIRE Regiment

Place	Date JUNE 1917	Hour	Summary of Events and Information	Remarks and references to Appendices
Right Sub Sector FAUQUISSART Sector	1		Nothing to report	CWS
do	2		do	CWS
do	3		do	CWS
do	4		do	CWS
do	5		Battalion relieved by 1/8th Battalion W. York Rgt. and moved to LA GORGUE	CWS
LA GORGUE	6		Bathing and cleaning up.	CWS
do	7	11.5 pm	Training. A raid was carried out on the enemy's trenches opposite FAUQUISSART No.1. – 4 Officers & 87 O.R. – Capt. E WALLING in Command – (Lieut G. L. BOYES – 2/Lt. G D SEARLE – 2/Lt. W J S Moore.) Party returned to our trenches, having failed to find any of the enemy. We had no casualties.	CWS
		11.56 pm		
do	8		Training.	CWS
do	9		Relieved 1/8th Battn. W. York Rgt. in the FAUQUISSART (Right Sub Sector) Sector	CWS
do	10		Nothing to report	CWS
do	11		do	CWS
do	12		do	CWS
do	13		Relieved by 1/8th Battn. W. York Rgt. – Battn moved to LAVENTIE in Brigade Reserve.	CWS
LAVENTIE	14		Bathing etc.	CWS
	15		Training	CWS
	16		do	CWS

Army Form C. 2118.

WAR DIARY
or
INTELLIGENCE SUMMARY. 1/7th. Battalion WEST YORKSHIRE REGT.
(Erase heading not required.)

Instructions regarding War Diaries and Intelligence Summaries are contained in F. S. Regs., Part II. and the Staff Manual respectively. Title pages will be prepared in manuscript.

Place	Date 1917 JUNE	Hour	Summary of Events and Information	Remarks and references to Appendices
LAVENTIE	17		Relieved the 1/8th Battn. W. YORK Regt. in Right Sub Sector - FAUQUISART (1)	C/M
FAUQUISART(1)	18		Nothing to report	C/M
	19		do	C/M
	20			
	21			
	22		Relieved by 1/8th. W. YORK Regt. in Right Sub Sector - FAUQUISART (1) & moved its Brigade Support in the RUE du BACQUEROT LINE, relieving 1/5th. Battn. there.	Batt.
	23		Nothing to report.	Batt.
	24		- do -	Batt.
	25		- do -	Batt.
	26		Bathing	Batt.
	27		Nothing to report.	Batt.
	28		Relieved 1/8th. Battn. W. YORK. Regt. in Right Sub Sector - FAUQUISART (1)	Batt.
	29		Nothing to report.	Batt.
	30		- do -	Batt.

WD Utley Lt. Col.
Comdg. 1/7th. W.Yorks. Regt.

Vol 28

SECRET.

WAR DIARY.

OF

1/7th Batt. West Yorks Regt

FOR

July 1917.

Army Form C. 2118.

WAR DIARY
or
INTELLIGENCE SUMMARY.
(Erase heading not required.)

1/7th Battn. West Yorkshire Regt.

Instructions regarding War Diaries and Intelligence Summaries are contained in F. S. Regs., Part II. and the Staff Manual respectively. Title pages will be prepared in manuscript.

Place	Date 1917	Hour	Summary of Events and Information	Remarks and references to Appendices
Right Sub Sector FAUQUISSART	July 1		Nothing to report.	CMS
do	2		do	CMS
do	3	1 Am	Intense hostile bombardment of our front line with trench mortars & guns of various calibres lasting for 1½ hours and causing 13 casualties (including 1 officer dangerously wounded)	CMS CMS
do	4		Nothing to report	CMS
do	5		Battalion relieved by 1/8th W.York Regt & moved into Brigade Reserve at LAVENTIE	CMS
LAVENTIE	6		Cleaning up –	CMS
do	7		Training	CMS
do	8		do	CMS
do	9		do – Enemy shelled training area at 10.30 Am. wounding 8 O.R.	CMS
do	10		Battalion relieved by 15th Battn. P.E.F. moved to billets in ESTAIRES	CMS
ESTAIRES	11		Training	CMS
do	12		do	CMS
do	13		The Battalion – less A Coy, which remained at ESTAIRES – moved by TRAIN to ZOON PLAGE & marched to MARDYK Camp	CMS
MARDYK Camp	14		Inspections	CMS
do	15		Training	CMS
do	16		Battalion marched to Fort de DUNES	CMS
Fort de DUNES	17		In Coast Defence relieving 1/4 York. & Lancs. WELSH Rgt. and marched to COXYDE Battalion relieved by 1/6 Battn. WELSH Rgt. and marched to COXYDE	CMS

Army Form C. 2118.

WAR DIARY
or
INTELLIGENCE SUMMARY.
(Erase heading not required.)

1/7th Battalion WEST YORKSHIRE Regt.

Instructions regarding War Diaries and Intelligence Summaries are contained in F.S. Regs., Part II. and the Staff Manual respectively. Title pages will be prepared in manuscript.

Place	Date 1917 July	Hour	Summary of Events and Information	Remarks and references to Appendices
COXYDE	18		Battalion marched to RIBAILLET CAMP (R.35.d. Sheet 11) & relieved 15th Lancashire Fusiliers in Brig. Reserve.	Cas.
RIBAILLET CAMP.	19		Nothing to report	Cas.
do	20		do	Cas.
do	21		do	Cas.
do	22	11.30 P.M.	Battalion "Stood to" for S.O.S. Left Brigade – No developments. Intense Bombardment	Cas.
do	23	3.10 A.M.	do S.O.S. Right Co. left Sub-Sector do	Cas.
		5 A.M.	Battalion Stood down – Inkastomin	
do	24		Working parties –	Cas.
do	25	6 A.M.	2/7th Manchester Regt. arrived in camp & were accommodated by Battn.	Cas.
LEFT Sub Sector St GEORGES Sector	26	3.0 A.M.	Relieved 1/5th Battn. W. York Regt.	Cas.
do	27		Nothing to report	Cas.
do	28	10.40 P.M.	A raiding party of 2 platoons & 1 Stg. left our trenches to raid enemy trenches at N.24.a.8.4.20. (Belgium Sheet S.W. 12 – 20000) Officers – Lieut T.D.GRIFFITHS – 2/Lt G.D.2.u.c.co.	Cas.
		11.0 P.M.	Barrage opened (2 pdr line)	
		11.30 P.M.	Raiding party returned but were unable to obtain prisoners – Our casualties – 4. OR Killed – 2/Lt. 2 v.c.c. + wounded – 4. OR Missing believed killed. – Enemy casualties 6 or 7 killed recovered	
		12 Midnight	B.O.R. wounded; – 4. O.R. Missing, believed killed. – CEASE FIRE.	
do	29		Nothing to report – Steady shelling all day by both sides	Cas.
do	30	1.30 A.M.	Gas discharge on enemy's line by Special Co. R.E. Projectors – Moderate artillery retaliation	Cas.

M. Callaghan

1577 Wt. W10791/1773 50,000 1/15 D.D. & L. A.D.S.S./Forms/C. 2118.

Army Form C. 2118.

WAR DIARY
or
INTELLIGENCE SUMMARY.
(Erase heading not required.)

17th Battn. WEST YORKSHIRE Regt.

Place	Date	Hour	Summary of Events and Information	Remarks and references to Appendices
LEFT Subsection St GEORGE'S Sector	July 1917 30		Heavy Trench Mortars fired on Nun Avenue & Battn. HQ. from 6 A.M. – 9.45 P.M. Continuous shelling of back area by batt. scales all day.	O.W.B.
		8 P.M.	Trial Barrage – No reply by enemy.	
		9.30 P.M.	Enemy opened up heavy barrage on our front, support & Is also Battn. HQ.	
			"S.O.S." sent up by right Coy. – Enemy made no infantry attack.	
		10.5 P.M.	All quiet – A very quiet night after this	
do	31		Nothing to report	

C P Dettey Lt Col.
Commanding 17th Bn.
West Yorkshire Regiment.

Vol 29

SECRET.

WAR DIARY.

OF

1/7th Batt. West York Reg.t

FOR

August 1914.

Army Form C. 2118.

1/4th Bn W York WAR DIARY or INTELLIGENCE SUMMARY.
(Erase heading not required.)

Instructions regarding War Diaries and Intelligence Summaries are contained in F. S. Regs., Part II. and the Staff Manual respectively. Title pages will be prepared in manuscript.

Place	Date	Hour	Summary of Events and Information	Remarks and references to Appendices
Left Sub Sector St Georges Sector	August 1st.	3 a.m.	German trenches were raided by us & casualties inflicted on the enemy. No prisoners were taken. Two platoons took part in the raid; one platoon of B. Coy. led by 2nd Lt. W.F.L. JOHNSON, & one platoon of D. Coy. led by Lt. T.D. GRIFFITHS. 2nd Lt. W.F.L. JOHNSON was wounded.	Plot.
– do –	1st.		On the night of the 1st/2nd. the battalion was relieved in trenches by 16th. Battn. Lancashire Fusiliers. The battn. then marched to billets in OOST DUNKERKE.	Plot.
Oost Dunkerke	2nd.		The battalion arrived in billets at about 3 a.m. & set off again for GHYVELDE at 6 p.m. arriving in billets at 11 p.m.	Plot.
Ghyvelde	3rd.		At 9.40 a.m. the march was recommenced, the destination being TETEGHAM, via UXEM. The battn. was inspected by the G.O.C. at the starting point GHYVELDE. Destination was reached at 12.30 p.m.	Plot.
Teteghem	4th.		The day was spent in cleaning-up & rest.	Plot.
– do –	5th.		Church parade & interior economy.	Plot.
– do –	6th.		Training in sand dunes N. of ROSENDAEL, also bathing.	Batt.
– do –	7th.		– do –	Batt.
– do –	8th.		– do –	Batt.
– do –	9th.		The battalion was inspected on the sands by the Corps Lieutenant General Sir J.P. Du Cane, K.C.B., Cmdg. XVth. Corps Commander,	Batt.
– do –	10th.		Training in sand dunes.	Batt.
– do –	11th.		– do –	Plot.
– do –	12th.		Church parade, physical training, interior economy.	Plot.

WAR DIARY or INTELLIGENCE SUMMARY

Army Form C. 2118.

Place	Date	Hour	Summary of Events and Information	Remarks and references to Appendices
TETEGHEM	August 13th		Training in Sand dunes.	Plott.
do	14th		Battalion in the Rifle Range E. of FORT/DUNES.	Plott.
do	15th		Training in Sand dunes & Bathing in the sea.	
do	16th		On this date the French civilian baths committee of ROSENDALE very kindly put these baths at our disposal & the day was spent in bathing & interior economy.	Plott.
do	17th		Training in the Sand dunes.	Plott.
do	18th		Battalion in the Rifle Range. Training Area.	Plott.
do	19th		Church Parades. Physical Training & Kit inspection	Plott.
do	20th		Training in Sand dunes. also Sea Bathing	Plott.
do	21st		Progressive training for A+C Coys. B+D Coys engaged in the construction of a new rifle range.	Plott.
do	22nd		Training in sand dunes.	Plott.
do	23rd		Two companies firing in the range, remainder usual training.	Plott.
do	24th		Training in Sand dunes.	Plott.
do	25th		Battn. Practise attack over the dunes, in presence of B.O.C. Brigade	Plott.
do	26th		Church Parade. Training & interior economy.	Plott.
do	27th		Training	Plott.
do	28th		Battalion moved to GHYVELDE via training area - attack practised in presence of G.O.C. Division, who complimented us on the display.	Plott.
GHYVELDE	29th		Training in ---- area - the day was too wet to go out.	Plott.

Army Form C. 2118.

WAR DIARY
or
INTELLIGENCE SUMMARY.
(Erase heading not required.)

Place	Date	Hour	Summary of Events and Information	Remarks and references to Appendices
GHYVELDE	Aug 30th		Training on Sand dunes — Specialist Training being the great feature of the work.	Batt.
	31st		ditto	Batt.

C.P. Ottery Lt. Col.
Comdg. 1/7th W. York Regt.

War Diary
of
17th Batt West Yorks Reg
for
September 1917

96 30

Secret

Army Form C. 2118.

WAR DIARY
or
INTELLIGENCE SUMMARY.
(Erase heading not required.)

17th. Battalion (PWO) WEST YORKSHIRE

Place	Date	Hour	Summary of Events and Information	Remarks and references to Appendices
GHYVELDE	Sept 1917 1		Training	CWS
do	2		Church Parade	CWS
do	3		Training – Battalion Sports	CWS
do	4		do	CWS
do	5		do	CWS
do	6		do	CWS
do	7		do – Battalion in the attack –	CWS
do	8		do	CWS
do	9		Church Parade	CWS
do	10		Training	CWS
do	11		do	CWS
do	12		do	CWS
do	13		do	CWS
do	14		do	CWS
do	15		do Church Parade	CWS
do	16		Church Parade	CWS
do	17		Training	CWS
do	18		do	CWS
do	19		do – Brigade in the attack	CWS
do	20		do	CWS
do	21		do – Brigade in the attack	CWS
do	22		Church Parade	CWS
do	23			CWS

Army Form C. 2118.

WAR DIARY
or
INTELLIGENCE SUMMARY.   1/7th Batn. (P.W.O.) West Yorkshire Regt.
(Erase heading not required.)

Place	Date Septem.	Hour	Summary of Events and Information	Remarks and references to Appendices
GHYVELDE	24		Battalion marched to billets at TETEGHEM.	CMS
TETEGHEM	25		do at WORMHOUDT	CMS
WORMHOUDT	26		do at OCHTEZEELE	CMS
OCHTEZEELE	27		Training	CMS
do	28		Battalion marched to LONGUENESSE (2 Companies in Camp – 2 Coys ppo in billets)	CMS
LONGUENESSE	29		2 Brigade practice attack. Battalion – interim enemy.	CMS
do	30		2 Brigades in a practice attack (146 + 148 Brigades)	CMS

CPDetley Lt Col
Commdg. 1/7 West Yorkshire Regiment.

WA 31

SECRET.

WAR DIARY.

OF

1st Auckland Infantry Regt

FOR

1st to 31st October 1917

Army Form C. 2118.

WAR DIARY
or
INTELLIGENCE SUMMARY.   17th Battn. (P.W.O) West Yorkshire Regt.
(Erase heading not required.)

Instructions regarding War Diaries and Intelligence Summaries are contained in F. S. Regs., Part II. and the Staff Manual respectively. Title pages will be prepared in manuscript.

Place	Date	Hour	Summary of Events and Information	Remarks and references to Appendices
LONGUENESS	Oct 1917 1		Battalion marched to billets in TERDEGHEM Area.	ans
TERDEGHEM	2		Resting - Interior economy	ans
do	3		Battalion marched to SHRINE Camp WATOU No. 2 Area	ans
SHRINE CAMP WATOU	4		Training	ans
do	5		do	ans
do	6		Moved to VLAMERTINGHE No 2 Area by bus	ans
VLAMERTINGHE	7		2 Officers + 8 O.R. per Coy. proceeded to the line on reconnaissance – Battalion completed equipment.	ans
do	8	7.30 A.M	Battalion marched to BRYKE, N. of YPRES (map HAZEBROUCK 5A) where it rested.	ans
BRYKE	8	5 P.M	Battalion assembled & proceeded by No. 6 Track to Assembly Position for attack	ans
CALGARY GRANGE	9	3 A.M	Battalion formed up in Assembly Positions N.E. of CALGARY GRANGE	ans
do		5.20 A.M	Attack commenced – vide narrative attached.	ans
do	10	10 P.M	Relief of Battalion by the 4th Battn. 3rd New Zealand Rifle Bde. commenced	ans
do	11	3 A.M	Relief complete	ans
NIELTJE		6 A.M	Battalion bivouacked in old British front line S. of WIELTJE	ans
		11.30 A.M	Battalion moved into huts at VLAMERTINGHE No 2 Area	ans
VLAMERTINGHE	12	2.45 P.M	Battalion embussed & moved to WINNEZEELE No 3 Area & encamped in "C" Camp near OUDEZEELE	ans

1577 Wt. W10791/1773 500,000 1/15 D. D. & L.   A.D.S.S./Forms/C. 2118.

Army Form C. 2118.

WAR DIARY
or
INTELLIGENCE SUMMARY.
(Erase heading not required.)

1/7k Bn. P.w.O. West Yorkshire Regt.

Place	Date	Hour	Summary of Events and Information	Remarks and references to Appendices
OUDEZEELE	13		Kit inspection, cleaning up etc.	CMS
do	14		Church Parade — Address to the Battalion by the Commanding Officer.	CMS
do	15		Training	CMS
do	16		do Rathing	CMS
do	17		Inspection of 1/146 Bde by Corps Commander	CMS
do	18		Training — Brigadier G.A.P. RENNIE D.S.O assumed Command of 146th Infantry Brigade vice Brigadier General M.D. Goring Jones C.M.G who proceeded to England on that date.	CMS
do	19		Training	CMS
do	20		do	CMS
do	21		Church Parade	CMS
do	22		Training	CMS
do	23		do.	CMS
do	24		do.	CMS
do	25		do.	CMS
do	26		do.	CMS
do	27		do.	CMS

Army Form C. 2118.

WAR DIARY
or
INTELLIGENCE SUMMARY. 19th Battn (P.W.O) West Yorkshire Regt

(Erase heading not required.)

Instructions regarding War Diaries and Intelligence Summaries are contained in F. S. Regs., Part II. and the Staff Manual respectively. Title pages will be prepared in manuscript.

Place	Date 1917 Oct.	Hour	Summary of Events and Information	Remarks and references to Appendices
OUDEZEELE	28		Battalion marched to billets in the EAST STEENVOORDE AREA.	C.W.S.
EAST STEENVOORDE AREA.	29		Training	C.W.S.
do	30		do	C.W.S.
do	31		do	C.W.S.

C.A.Cutts,
Lieut. Colonel.
Commanding 1/9th Bn (P.W.O) West Yorkshire Regt.

Narrative of Recent Operations.

The battalion assembled at LA BRIQUE at 9 a.m. on Oct. 8th & at 5 p.m. started to move up No. 6 track to the assembly position. The night was very dark & rain commenced to fall shortly before 5 p.m. & continued during the night, making the march up to CALGARY GRANGE very difficult, many parts of the track being almost impossible to follow; shortly after leaving the ST. JULIEN Road it was found that all the trench grids had been removed for a considerable distance.

The head of the battalion reached CALGARY GRANGE about midnight & the whole Battalion was in position by 3.0 a.m. on Oct. 9th.; the men were all very tired. There was a certain amount of shelling on the way up but no casualties occurred until the Battalion reached the assembly position.

The barrage opened at 5.20 a.m.; the troops were all ready & advanced at once; owing however to the broken ground, which was very wet & soft,

2.

& to the water in the STROOMBEEK, the troops did not keep up to the barrage at first, but I think that they got up to it again before reaching the first objective.

The companies at first kept rather too much to the right in the direction of PETER PAN but they afterward changed direction & passed YETTA HOUSES at about the proper distance. Battn. H.Q. moved forward behind the companies & took up a position in shell holes ~~about 150 yards~~ near CALGARY GRANGE.

No news was received from companies until Lt. BALDWIN, M.C., O.C. Left Coy. for second objective, came back wounded about 7 a.m. & said that his company was held up by a machine gun fire & snipers fire from the left as soon as they moved forward through the 1st objective companies; he told me that he had given orders that 2 platoons should move along to deal with this M.G. but they apparently failed to silence this gun.

As I got no reports whatever from

the companies I went up to the front line myself near YETTA HOUSES & found that B3 companies were consolidating there with their left about 100x from YETTA HOUSES The men were too crowded & I gave orders that the men of one company were to be collected & taken to some trenches further in rear. The other company (the right coy: for the 1st objective) was nearer PETER PAN where it was in touch with the 1/5th Bn. W. York. Rgt.

Two officers were left on duty with my right company, but in the other 3 coys all the officers & the greater part of the senior N.C.O's had become casualties. this made it difficult to obtain really reliable information. Enemy M. Guns & snipers in carefully concealed positions were very active; they continued to fire through the barrage & were able to prevent our advance to the second objective owing to the accuracy of their fire & the difficulty of locating their exact positions. A number of the enemy were killed by our rifle & Lewis Gun fire & an enemy machine gun firing from the parapet of a trench on the right, &

enfilading troops advancing on the left
was rushed by one man singlehanded,
whereupon the team ran away; as
the man found that he could not
work the gun he disabled it.

During the morning of Oct. 9th
Capt. MANBER with 2 coys. of the 1/4th.
W. Riding Rgt. reported to me & at 2.0 p.m.
I sent one of these companies to YETTA
HOUSES to fill the gap between the left
of my line & the right of the 1/8th.
W. Yorks. Rgt.

Small counter attacks were
attempted by the enemy about 2 p.m. &
6 p.m. but these came to nothing.
At 10.30 p.m. on Oct. 9th I received
instructions that a company of the 1/6th
~~Bn. W. Yorks. Rgt~~ Bn. W. Riding Rgt. would
mop up the area between my line &
the most advanced posts.
Lt. Col. BATEMAN of the 1/6th. W. Riding Rgt.
made his H.Q. at CALGARY GRANGE.
(N.B. During the morning of Oct. 9th I moved
my batn. H.Q. back to CALGARY GRANGE
as the shell hole position was too indefinite
for gunners to find)

Early in the morning of Oct. 10th the O.C.
the 1/6th. W. Riding Rgt. mopping-up coy:

reported that his company had covered all the ground up to the post held by my right coy. There Lt. MOORE informed him that he was in the most advanced position of the Battn; he therefore considered that he had carried out his instructions.

During the night of the 9th/10th, I sent first my Intelligence Officer & afterwards my Regt. Sgt. Major to ascertain the position in the front line. Both were wounded, however, & I had no one else to send at the time.

At 6 a.m. on Oct. 10th I sent my Signalling Officer up to the front line; he reported that all was quiet & in order.

The first companies of the relieving Battn. of the New Zealand Rifles came up about 9 p.m. & relief was complete about midnight.

Enemy shelling was heavy throughout the day of Oct 10th & during the relief, & the New Zealand Rifles suffered a good many casualties.

C.H. Dilley
Lt. Col.
Comdg 1/7 Bn. W. York. Regt. (T.F.)

13/10/17.

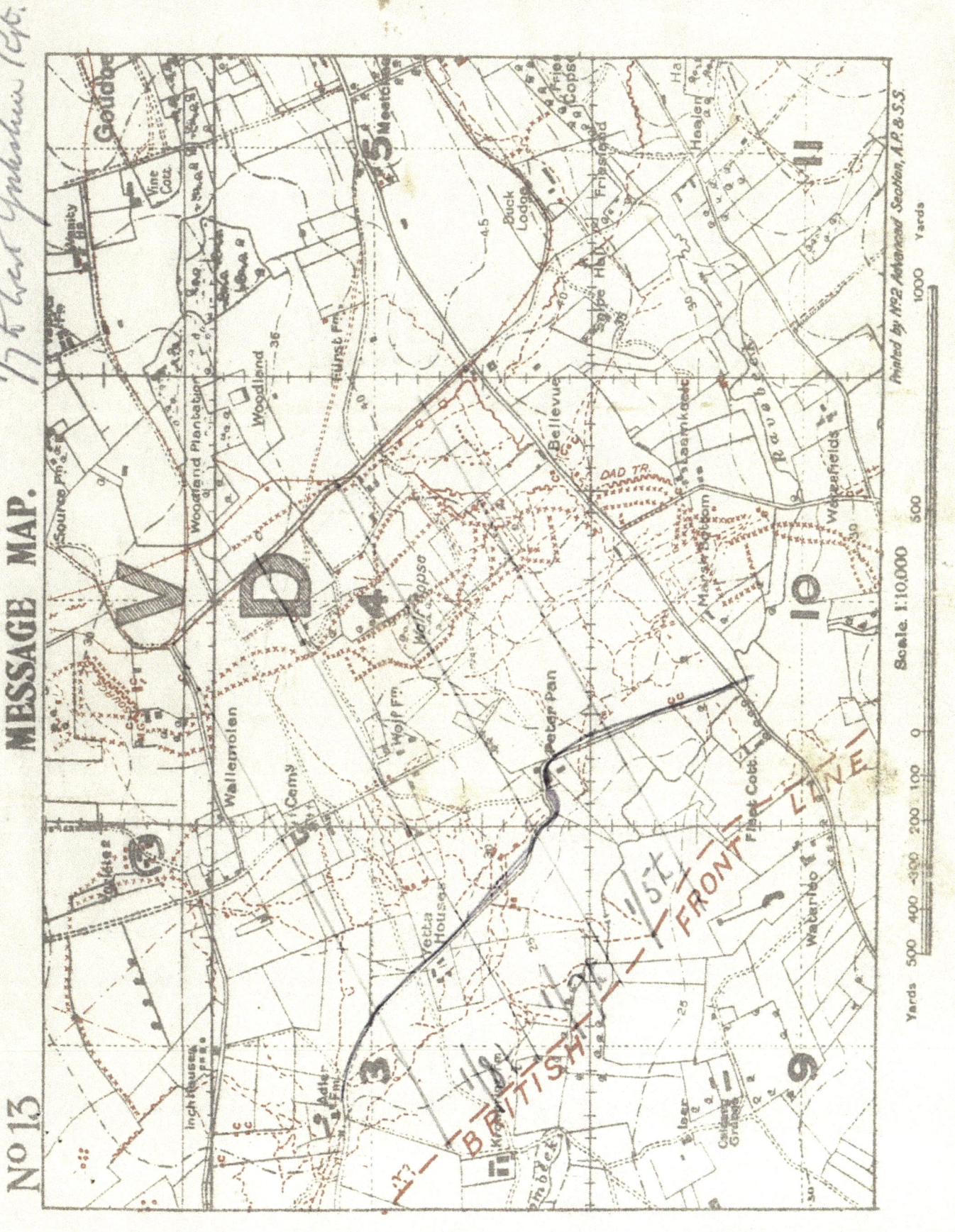

MESSAGE FORM.

To:— No.

1. I am at........................ (Note:—Either give Map Reference or mark your position by a 'X' on the Map on back.)

2. I have reached limits of my Objective.

3. My Platoon / Company is at........................and is consolidating.

4. My Platoon / Company is at........................and has consolidated.

5. Am held up by (a) M.G. (b) Wire at........................(Place where you are).

6. Enemy holding strong point........................

7. I am in touch with........................on Right / Left. at........................

8. I am not in touch with........................on Right / Left.

9. Am shelled from........................

10. Am in need of :—

11. Counter Attack forming at........................

12. Hostile (a) Battery
    (b) Machine Gun   active at........................
    (c) Trench Mortar

13. Reinforcements wanted at........................

14. I estimate my present strength at........................rifles.

15. Add any other useful information here :—

Name........................
Platoon........................
Time............m. Company........................
Date............1917. Battalion........................

(A). Carry no maps or papers which may be of value to the Enemy.

(B). Give no information if captured, except the following, which you are bound to give :—
    Name and Rank.

(C). Collect all captured maps and papers and send them in at once.

WO 32

1st/49

Confidential.

War Diary

of

1/4th Battalion (P.W.O.) West Yorkshire Regiment (T.F.)

From Nov 1st 1917 to Nov 30th 1917.

, 2118.

WAR DIARY
or
INTELLIGENCE SUMMARY.
(Erase heading not required.)

1/5 Bn. (P.W.O.) West Yorkshire Regt (T.F.)

Instructions regarding War Diaries and Intelligence Summaries are contained in F. S. Regs., Part II. and the Staff Manual respectively. Title pages will be prepared in manuscript.

Place	Date	Hour	Summary of Events and Information	Remarks and references to Appendices
EAST STEENVOORDE	1917 Nov. 1		Training — Gen. Plumer visited the Battalion & walked round the Training area.	CWS
	2		Training	CWA
	3		do	CW
	4		Church Parade	CW
	5		Training	CW
	6		do	CW
	7		do — Battalion attack.	CW
	8		Battalion moved to Shelters in front of YPRES	CWA
YPRES	9		Cleaning up & Preparation for moving into the lines.	CWS
	10		— do —	CWS
	11		Bn. moved into the line — Relieving the 23rd Battn. Australian Infantry as Right Front Line Battalion.	CWS
			Nothing to report	CW
WESTHOEK	12		do	CW
Sector	13		do	CWS
	14		Battalion on relief by 1/8 Bn. W. York. Regt. moved in Support Position as Right Support	CW
	15		Battalion in Pill Boxes & Shelters on ANZAC Ridge	

WAR DIARY
or
INTELLIGENCE SUMMARY.
(Erase heading not required.)

1/7th Battalion (P.W.O.) West Yorkshire Regt. (T.F.)

Place	Date Mar	Hour	Summary of Events and Information	Remarks and references to Appendices
ANZAC Ridge WESTHOEK	16		Carrying parties - Work in Shelters	CWB
do	17		do	CM
do	18		do	CM
do	19	2pm	Relieved by 1/4th Battn. (D.W.) West Riding Regt. - On relief Battalion moved into Camp in SWAN AREA in Divisional Support Brigade Area WEST of YPRES.	CM
SWAN Area W. of YPRES	20	12 Noon	Battalion relieved by 1/4th Battn. York and Lancaster Regt. (Hallamshires) + moved into Divisional Reserve near DICKEBUSCH	CM
DICKEBUSCH	21		Cleaning up - Kit Inspection etc.	CM
do	22		Training	CM
do	23		do	CM
do	24		do	Battalion moved to HALIFAX CAMP S.E. of YLAMERTINGHE	CM
HALIFAX Camp	25		Church Parade - Battalion performance at Cinema.	CM
do	26		Training	CM
do	27		do	CM
do	28		Battalion moved to POTIJZE (Dragoon Farm Camp) "Brigade in Support"	CM
POTIJZE	29		Working parties	CM

WAR DIARY
or
INTELLIGENCE SUMMARY.

1/7th Battalion (P.W.O) West Yorkshire Regt (T.F.)

(Erase heading not required.)

Instructions regarding War Diaries and Intelligence Summaries are contained in F. S. Regs., Part II. and the Staff Manual respectively. Title pages will be prepared in manuscript.

Place	Date 1917	Hour	Summary of Events and Information	Remarks and references to Appendices
POTIJZE	Nov. 30		Working Parties	C.W.B.

C.W. Sullivorale
Major.
Commanding 1/7th Battn (P.W.O) West Yorkshire Regt.

146/49

Vol 33

Secret.

War Diary of
14th Bn. A.I.F. Yorks R.

From Dec 1-19-17
Dec 31-19-17

WAR DIARY
or
INTELLIGENCE SUMMARY. 1/7th Battalion (P.W.O) West Yorkshire Regt.

Army Form C. 2118.

Place	Date 1917	Hour	Summary of Events and Information	Remarks and references to Appendices
POTIJZE	Dec. 1		Working Parties	CMS
	2		do	CMS
	3		do	CMS
	4		Training, Foot-washing, preparation for trenches	CMS
	5		Battalion relieved the 1/5 R.O.Y.L.I. in the Right Sub Sector WESTHOEK Sector (Pontius)	CMS
WESTHOEK Sector	6		Patrols reconnoitred CELTIC WOOD & JUSTICE WOOD – Nothing to report	CMS
do	7		Patrols reconnoitred FLINTE FME and house and also CELTIC WOOD – Nothing to report	CMS
do	8		Battalion on relief by 1/8th Bn. 6. Yorks Regt. Moved to GARTER POINT & vicinity as Reser- Support Battalion.	CMS
GARTER POINT	9		Working Parties	Nutt
do	10		do	
do	11		On relief by 1/6th Yorks Lancs. the Battn. moved out to Canal Area W. of YPRES Battn. H.Q. in Belgian Chateau	Nutt
CANAL AREA NEAR YPRES	12		Working Parties	Nutt
do	13		do	Nutt
do	14		do	Nutt

WAR DIARY
or
INTELLIGENCE SUMMARY.

(Erase heading not required.)

1/7th Battalion (P.W.O.) West Yorkshire Regt.

Army Form C. 2118.

Place	Date	Hour	Summary of Events and Information	Remarks and references to Appendices
CANAL AREA NEAR YPRES	September 1917 15		Working parties	Cas
do	16		Battery return economy	Cas
do	17		Relieved 1/4th Duke of Wellington's West Riding Regt. in left sector, near VEER FME.	Cas
Pill Sebastion VEER FME.	18		Nothing to report – being patrolled	Cas
do	19		do	Cas
do	20		do	Cas
do	21		do	Cas
do	22		do	Cas
do	23		do – Relieved by 1/8 bryok Bt moved to support position at ANZAC House	Cas
ANZAC House	24		Working Parties.	Batt
	25		do	Batt
	26		do.	Batt
	27		do.	Batt
	28		do	Batt
	29		Battn. relieved by 1/4th Bn. K.O.Y.L.I. – moved to POTIJZE, E. of YPRES.	Batt
POTIJZE	30		Battn. moved to VANCOUVER CAMP – west of YPRES. Lt. Col. C.H. TETLEY, D.S.O. takes over temporary command of 146th Inf Brigade during absence of B.G.C. (on leave)	Batt
VANCOUVER CAMP	31		Bathing	Batt

A.V. Braithwaite

Major
Comdg. 1/7th Bn. W. Yorks. Regt.

CONFIDENTIAL.

WAR DIARY

of

1/7th Bn. West Yorkshire Regt.

From - 1-1-18   To - 31-1-18.

Army Form C. 2118.

WAR DIARY
or
INTELLIGENCE SUMMARY.

(Erase heading not required.)

1/7? Bn. N° P.W.O (West Yorkshire Regt) T.F.

Place	Date 1918 Jan.	Hour	Summary of Events and Information	Remarks and references to Appendices
VANCOUVER CAMP.	1		Working parties.	Orders.
"	2		do.	Matt.
"	3		do.	Matt.
"	4		Battn. moved into trenches at MOLENAARELSTHOEK taking over from 1/5th. W. Riding Rgt.	Matt.
"	5		A fairly quiet day. Patrols were sent out but no enemy were encountered	Batt.
"	6		do.	Matt.
"	7		Some heavy shelling but few casualties.	Matt.
"	8		Battn. was relieved in trenches by the 1/8th Bn. W. York. Rgt., & moved into Brigade Reserve at DRAGOON CAMP, POTIZE.	Matt.
DRAGOON CAMP.	9		Working Parties	Batt.
"	10		do.	Batt.
"	11		do.	Batt.
"	12		do.	Batt.
"	13		Batt. moved into G.H.Q. Reserve, in billets near STAPLE, being relieved by the 2/7? Manchester Regiment.	Batt.
STAPLE.	14		Refitting &c.	Batt.
"	15		do	Batt.
"	16		Training.	Batt.
"	17		do	Batt.

Army Form C. 2118.

WAR DIARY
or
INTELLIGENCE SUMMARY.
(Erase heading not required.)

Place	Date	Hour	Summary of Events and Information	Remarks and references to Appendices
STAPLE	Apr 18		Training	Pratt
	19		do	Pratt
	20		Sports Church Parade + Kit Inspection	Pratt
	21		Bathing	Pratt
	22		Training	Pratt
	23		do	Pratt
	24		do	Pratt
	25		Training. Be lecture by B.E.O.	Pratt
	26		Batn Outpost Scheme.	Pratt
	27		Church Parade + Kit Inspection	Pratt
	28		Training - Including firing on the Range.	Pratt
	29		do. - Range Practice + Bayonet fighting.	Pratt
	30		do. - Demonstration of Flame Projector. Bathing.	Pratt
	31		Training + Bathing. Brigade Cross Country Run	Pratt

31/1/18.

C.W.Ottley Lt. Col.
Cmdg. 1/7th. Bn. W. York. Rgt.

Vol 35

Confidential

WAR DIARY

1/7th Batt (P.W.O) West Yorkshire Regt

1/2/18 — 28/2/18

Army Form C. 2118.

WAR DIARY
or
INTELLIGENCE SUMMARY.

(Erase heading not required.)

1/5th Battn. P.W.O. West Yorkshire Regt. T.F.

Place	Date 1918 Feby.	Hour	Summary of Events and Information	Remarks and references to Appendices
STAPLE	1		Moved to HOULLE Area for Musketry	C/M
HOULLE	2		Musketry on B. Range	C/M
do	3		do	C/M
do	4		do	C/M
do	5		Battalion moved to STAPLE Area	C/M
STAPLE	6		Revisional Training. The Brigade Rifles Brigade Contest was won by 'C' Coy.	1 Statt. C/M
do	7		do	C/M
do	8		do	C/M
do	9		do – B. Coy. won the 146 Bde – Company Drill Competition. D Coy. won the S.B.R. Competition	C/M
do	10		Church Parade – The Battn. won the Bde. Final Association Football Match v. 1/5th W. Yorks.	C/M
do	11		Battalion moved to RENINGHELST Area for work on Corps line.	C/M
MONTREAL CAMP-BRANDHOEK	12		Working on Corps line – in the district of ZONNEBEKE	Plat.
do	13		do	Plat.
	14		do	Plat.
	15		do	Plat.
	16		do	Plat.
	17		do	Plat.
	18		do	Plat.
	19		do	Plat.

Army Form C. 2118.

WAR DIARY
or
INTELLIGENCE SUMMARY.
(Erase heading not required.)

Instructions regarding War Diaries and Intelligence Summaries are contained in F.S. Regs., Part II. and the Staff Manual respectively. Title pages will be prepared in manuscript.

Place	Date	Hour	Summary of Events and Information	Remarks and references to Appendices
MONTREAL Camp BRANDHOEK	20		Working on Cntr Line - in the district of ZONNEBEKE	1 Platt
	21		do	1 Platt
	22		do	1 Platt
	23		The battn. moved into the line, taking over a brigade frontage in front of YPRES. Battn. H.Q. at RETALIATION FARM. Attempted enemy raid on night 23rd/24th resulting in the capture of 15 prisoners by us. (See Appendix)	1 Platt
	24		A quiet day in the line.	1 Platt
	25		do	1 Platt
	26		do	1 Platt Coy H.Q. M
	27		Moved into support.	
	28		Support. (Brigade).	

J.J. Moore Lieut.
for Lt. Col.
Comdg. 1/1 Bn. Prn. W. York Regt.

Attempted enemy raid on the trenches held by the 1/7 W. YORK Reg. on the BROODSEINDE Ridge on the night of the 23rd/24th Feby 1918.

At 11.20 pm the enemy opened a heavy barrage on the front & support lines along the whole Battalion front. At the same time a strong enemy party approached our advanced post at D.23.d.50.50 - This post was manned by Corporal Moss (D. Coy) and 8 O.R. who estimated the enemy to have been nearly 100 strong. The post immediately opened fire with Lewis gun & rifles and the enemy attempted to surround them and commenced to throw stick bombs. After putting up as strong a resistance as possible, and being in imminent danger of getting cut off & captured Cpl. Moss decided to withdraw his party to the front line posts. This he succeeded in doing. By this time he had had two men killed and two wounded.

In the centre of the front the enemy seems to have made no attempt to enter our line.

On the Right Coy's front more of the enemy were seen by our sentries and a party of 1 Officer and 15 OR were successful in crossing our front line near D.29.d.45.40. The first indication of their presence was when Capt. Booth (B Coy) on proceeding down N.10.D Commun. Trench met a German running towards him and captured him.

The remainder of the enemy party then apparently crossed the C.T. and proceeded towards our No 2 Support post. Capt. Roberts (A Coy) was here and ordered Lewis Gun & rifle fire to be opened from the post at the same time sending Sgt. Sanderson (C Coy) and some men up the C.T. to work round and cut off the enemy's retreat. It was here that the German officer was wounded and one of his men killed, the remainder were captured by Sgt. Sanderson & his party.

Confidential

Vol 36
146/49

WAR DIARY
of
1/7th. Bn. (P.W.O.) W. York. Regt.
1/3/18 — 31/3/18.

Army Form C. 2118.

WAR DIARY
or
INTELLIGENCE SUMMARY.
(Erase heading not required.) 1/7th Batn. 3rd/4th West Yorkshire Regt. T.F.

Place	Date 1918 March	Hour	Summary of Events and Information	Remarks and references to Appendices
GARTER POINT	1		Nothing to report - bombing parties	CWS
do	2		do	CWS
do	3		Battalion relieved by 1/6 W. York Regt. & moved to Hussar Camp - Bde. Reserve	CWS
HUSSAR CAMP POTIJZE	4		Salvaging	CWS
do	5		do	CWS
do	6		do	
do	7		Battalion moved into the line - H.Q. Retaliation Farm - relieved the 1/5th. Bn. W. York. Regt.	Vett.
LEFT Sector BRODSEINDE do Reg	8		Nothing to report.	Vett. Vett.
do	9		do	Vett. Vett.
do	10		do	Vett.
do	11			
GARTER POINT	12		Battn. moved to GARTER POINT after being relieved by the 1/6th. Bn. W. york. Regt.	Vett. Vett.
do	13		do Refmt - Working Parties	Vett. Vett.
do	14		do	Vett.
do	15		Battn. relieved by 1/6th. Bn. W. York Regt. & moved to Brigade reserve at HUSSAR CAMP, POTIJZE.	Vett.
HUZZAR CAMP.	16		Salvaging	CWS
do	17		do	CWS

WAR DIARY
or
INTELLIGENCE SUMMARY.
(Erase heading not required.)

Army Form C. 2118.

1/7th Battn. P.S.O. West Yorkshire Rgt. T.F.

Place	Date	Hour	Summary of Events and Information	Remarks and references to Appendices
	March 1918			
HUZZAR Camp POTIJZE	18		Salvaging	CW
do	19		Battalion relieved 1/5th Battn. W York Rgt. in the front line – ZONNEBEKE SECTOR	CW
LEFT Sector	20		Nothing to report	CW
BROODSEINDE RIDGE	21		do	CW
do	22		do	CW
do	23		do – Battalion on relief by 1/6th York Rgt. moved to EXETER POINT and relieved	CW
EXETER Pt.	24		1/5 Battn. W York as Battalion in Brigade Support	CW
do	25		do (working parties)	CW
do	26		do	CW
do	27		do	CW
MOLENAARELSTHOEK	28		Relieved 1/6 Battn W York Rgt in the trenches – "MDL" SECTOR	CW
do	29		Nothing to Report. 2/Lt. W. WHEELTON, M. in A. whilst on patrol into Adams Road.	MDA
do	30		The Battn. relieved in due time by 1st. BUFFS, moved out to WEST FARM CAMP, POTIJZE.	MDA
WEST FARM CAMP	31		Interior Economy. Camp shelled during afternoon causing casualties. Bathing.	MDA

WDUttley
Lt. Col.
Comdg. 1/7th Bn. W Yorks Regt.

146th Brigade.

49th Division.

1/7th BATTALION

WEST YORKSHIRE REGIMENT

APRIL 1918.

Attached :-

Report on Operations 10th-16th April 1918.

Army Form C. 2118.

WAR DIARY
or
INTELLIGENCE SUMMARY.
(Erase heading not required.)

Instructions regarding War Diaries and Intelligence Summaries are contained in F. S. Regs, Part II. and the Staff Manual respectively. Title pages will be prepared in manuscript.

Place	Date	Hour	Summary of Events and Information	Remarks and references to Appendices
WEST FARM CAMP	1918 APRIL 1st.		The batn. moved into the line of hold TOWER HAMLET relieving	Matt.
TOWER HAMLETS	2nd.		A quiet day - nothing to report.	Matt.
	3rd.		do.	Matt.
	4th.		do.	Matt.
	5th.		The batn. moved to tunnel at TOR TOP, JACKDAW & CLAPHAM JUNCTION after relief by 1/4th York & Lancs Regt. on night of 5th/6th.	Matt.
TOR TOP	6th.		The batn. moved into the lines relieving the 7th. W. Riding Regt. in the CAMERON Sector on the night 6th/7th.	Matt.
CAMERON Sector	7th.		A quiet day.	Matt.
do	8th.		do. Nothing to report.	
do	9th.		The batn. was relieved in the line by 1st. Bn. P.W.O. (W. Yorks. Regt.) on night of the 9th/10th. inst. & moved to billets in LANKHOF CAMP.	Matt.
LANKHOF CAMP	10th		Camp Shelled - some casualties. The batn. moved by light railway to CHIPPEWA CAMP.	Matt.
CHIPPEWA CAMP	"		At about 9 p.m. orders received to move at once to PARRET CAMP (near KEMMEL) there reporting to the 62nd. Inf. Brigade at whose disposal the batn. was to be until	Matt.

1577 Wt. W10791/1773 500,000 1/15 D. D. & L. A.D.S.S./Forms/C. 2118.

Army Form C. 2118.

WAR DIARY
or
INTELLIGENCE SUMMARY.
(Erase heading not required.)

Instructions regarding War Diaries and Intelligence Summaries are contained in F. S. Regs., Part II. and the Staff Manual respectively. Title pages will be prepared in manuscript.

Place	Date	Hour	Summary of Events and Information	Remarks and references to Appendices
			2/	
	10th		orders. Although the troops were exceedingly tired the march was carried out with in a splendid style & at about 4 a.m all were in billets at LINCOLN CAMP (about 600x N of PARRET CAMP).	Nott.
LINCOLN CAMP	11th 4.4.34		The Battn. received orders to move into the line immediately to form a defensive flank S. of WYTSCHAETE. D & C Coys formed a defensive flank in O.4.c. & O.25.a. (Sector). A&B Coys & Battn. H.Q. moved to REGENT Dugouts at N.29.O.4.4. — C.O. to WYTSCHAETE. (See attached letter from Gen. Ricc.)	Nott.
WYTSCHAETE	12th 2.10 am		A & B Coys. moved to positions in O.25.a. — O.4.c. — N.24.d. — N.30.a, b, c.	Nott.
		6 am	All Coys. in new position	
	13th		Clothing to refit	Nott.
	14th 6.5 am		Battn. H.Q. moved to IRISH HOUSE (ALBERTA DUG-OUTS - N.23.d.2.8.)	Nott.
	15th 10 pm		D Coy relieved by 1st Lincoln Regt. & moved into position in N.30.	Nott.
	16th 4 am		Heavy enemy barrage opened & enemy ATTACKED.	Nott.
	16th 8 am		Orders for 1 Battn. to move to SIEGE FARM received.	Nott.
	16th		Battn. H.Q. left IRISH HOUSE & established H.Q. at Farm in N.8.c.	Nott.
	16th		Farm in N.8.c. noting & reorganising - rejoined 146th Inf. Bde	Nott.

Army Form C. 2118.

WAR DIARY
or
INTELLIGENCE SUMMARY.
(Erase heading not required.)

Instructions regarding War Diaries and Intelligence Summaries are contained in F.S. Regs., Part II. and the Staff Manual respectively. Title pages will be prepared in manuscript.

Place	Date	Hour	Summary of Events and Information	Remarks and references to Appendices
FARM in N.2.6.	19th		Nothing to report.	Nott.
	20th		do.	Nott.
	21st		do.	Nott.
	22nd		do.	R/t. Nott.
	23rd		do.	Nott.
	24th		The Battn. (organised as one coy.) less H.Q. moved into the VIERSTRAAT LINE — in reserve to 1/5th & 1/6th W. Yorks. Regt.	Nott.
	25th 2am		Enemy barrage opened ab 6 a.m. We attacked.	Nott. Nott.
	25th 7pm		The Battn. was withdrawn from the line to a camp at OUDERDOM	W.t.
OUDERDOM	26th		A party of 1 officer (2nd Lt. HENDERSON) & 14 O.R. who were thought to be missing arrived.	Nott.
	27th		A similar party under 2nd Lt. FEATHER turned up.	Nott.
HOOGRAAF CAMP	28th		The Battn. (minus a composite coy. which had been attached to a composite Battn. formed of units of 146th Inf. Bde. & Comanded by Major Clough of (now 1/6th. W.Y.R.)) moved to a camp near HOOGRAAF CAMP.	Nott.
	29th		The Battn. (less composite coy. moved to a farm nr K.23.6.) (Sheet 27)	Nott. Nott.
	30th			

J. C. Taylor
Comdg. 1/7th Bn. W. York Rgt.

9th Division.

B.M. 65/62

62nd Infantry Brigade.

Holding of the WYTSCHAETE Sector 10/1 to 16th April 1918 and the attack and Counter-attacks on 16th April, 1918.

The accounts of the recent fighting in the WYTSCHAETE Sector as far as it affected the 1st and 2nd Battalions of the Lincolnshire Regiment and the 12/13 Northumberland Fusiliers are forwarded herewith.

I should like also to draw attention to the very gallant behaviour of the 1/7th West Yorkshire Regt. of the 146th Inf. Bde. and of No. 2 Composite Battalion, 39th Division who were attached to my Brigade.

On the critical afternoon of the 11th March [April?] when the Brigade holding the MESSINES Sector, was driven back leaving my right flank perilously exposed the 1/7th West Yorkshire Regt. was moved up at very short notice from PARRET CAMP to form a defensive flank on the BOGAERT FARM - PICKWOOD Spur and to fill the gap on our right.

Under very heavy shelling the battalion moved forward splendidly and their steadiness undoubtedly saved the situation. From that evening until the morning of the 16th the battalion held the Right Subsector of the Brigade front from BOGAERT FARM to PICKWOOD: on the night of the 15/16th they handed over from BOGAERT FARM to SCOTT FARM to the 1st Lincolnshire Regt. and took over to SPANBROEKMOLEN inclusive. On an extended front they encountered the full force of the enemy attack on the morning of the 16th and fought most gallantly until overwhelmed by superior numbers. As in the case of other battalions the mist placed them at an enormous disadvantage, and deprived them of the full use of their fire power.

The 2nd Composite Battalion, 39th Division, was placed under my orders on the night of the 15/16th, and was moved to ROSSIGNOL WOOD. On the morning of the 16th it was moved forward with the 2nd Lincolnshire Regiment to the line VANDAMME FARM - LAGACHE FARM - STORE FARM.

It took part in the counter-attack on the evening of the 16th to re-occupy MIDDELSTEDE FARM and WYTSCHAETE WOOD, advancing most gallantly under heavy machine gun fire, both enfilade and frontal, and securing their first objective. They were unable to advance further owing to the fact that no French attack developed on their right.

This battalion, during the counter-attacks, and subsequently in holding and consolidating the line, displayed great steadiness and gallantry under very adverse conditions, and with no previous knowledge and reconnaissance of the ground.

In estimating the achievements of the units under my command I should like to draw special attention to the following points :-

1. That except in the case of the 1/7th West Yorkshire Regt, more than half of the Battalions consisted of drafts, and that there had been no adequate time to re-organise before going into the line. Many of these drafts had not been in the line before and were youths under 20.

2. My own three battalions were very short of Officers, not more than two a Company when they were in: this number was diminished by casualties before the attack.

3. The Brigade was subjected to very heavy shelling for five days before the attack on the 16th.

4. That on the 16th there was practically no stragglers.

(sd) G.H.GATER, Brigadier General.
Commanding 62nd Infantry Brigade.

20/4/18.

Vol. 38

CONFIDENTIAL

WAR DIARY
of
1/7th Batt. P.W.O. (West Yorkshire) Regt.

1/5/18 — 31/5/18.

Army Form C. 2118.

WAR DIARY
or
INTELLIGENCE SUMMARY.
(Erase heading not required.) 1/4th Bn. P.W.O. West Yorkshire Regt (T.F.)

Place	Date	Hour	Summary of Events and Information	Remarks and references to Appendices
CAMP in R.E. (H.23)	1918 MAY 1st		Training & Reorganising.	
do	2nd		do.	
do	3rd		Bathing & Training.	
do	4th		Training	
do	5th		Bath. moved to Tunnellers Camp, St Jan Ter Biezen	
TUNNELLERS CAMP ST JAN TER BIEZEN	6th		Reorganisation int. coys.	
do	7th		do.	
do	8th		Training.	
do	9th		do & tattoo.	
do	10th		A.A. Protection Training. 2 Coys on Range.	
do	11th		Training & tattoo.	
do	12th		Training	
do	13th		do.	
do	14th		Inspection by General Plumer. Range. General Training.	
do	15th		Training	
do	16th		do - Musketry party - 5 Officers 90 O.R. to Casser for Range firing.	

Army Form C. 2118.

WAR DIARY
or
INTELLIGENCE SUMMARY.

(Erase heading not required.) 1/7th Battn. P.W.O. West Yorkshire Rgt. (T.F.)

Place	Date 1918	Hour	Summary of Events and Information	Remarks and references to Appendices
St. Jan Ter Biezen	May 17	Training		CDS
do	18	do		CDS
do	19	do	— Church Parade — Musketry party returned from Cassel	CDS
do	20	do		CDS
do	21	do		CDS
do	22	do		CDS
do	23	do		CDS
do	24	do		CDS
do	25	Battn.	Moved by train to St. Omer & marched to Muckety Camp near Cornette	CDS
Cornette	26	Firing on Range & Training		CDS
do	27	do		CDS
do	28	Field Firing		CDS
do	29	Range Firing		CDS
do	30	Sports. Battn. Parade		CDS
do	31	Moved by train to Proven Area		CDS

A. Dunbar Major
Commdg 1/7 W. York R.C.

Confidential

WAR DIARY
of
1/7th Bn. P.W.O. (W. York. Rgt.)
1/6/18 — 30/6/18.

VR 39

Army Form C. 2118.

WAR DIARY
or
INTELLIGENCE SUMMARY.
(Erase heading not required.)

1/7th Batt. P.W.O. West Yorkshire Rgt. T.F.

Place	Date	Hour	Summary of Events and Information	Remarks and references to Appendices
	1918 JUNE			
PROVEN	1		Training	App 8
do	2		Church Parade & Training	App 1
do	3		Battalion relieved 20th Batt. D.L.I. in Div. Reserve at 28/A.30.c.8.1 (BRAKE CAMP)	App 9
BRAKE CAMP	4		Training	App
do	5		Working parties Training	App
do	6		do	App
do	7		do	App
do	8		Training	App
do	9		Church Parade & Training	App
do	10		Training	App
do	11		The Battn. moved into Brigade Reserve around the ramparts of YPRES relieving 1/4 th. York & Lancs.	App
YPRES	12		Settling in to report.	App
	13		do	App
	14		do	App
	15		do	App

Army Form C. 2118.

WAR DIARY
or
INTELLIGENCE SUMMARY.
(Erase heading not required.)

Instructions regarding War Diaries and Intelligence Summaries are contained in F. S. Regs., Part II. and the Staff Manual respectively. Title pages will be prepared in manuscript.

Place	Date	Hour	Summary of Events and Information	Remarks and references to Appendices
YPRES	16		Nothing to report.	Rutt.
"	17		Battn. moved into the front-line E. of YPRES relieving 1/5th Bn. W. Yorks. Regt.	Rutt.
"	18		All quiet.	Rutt.
"	19		do.	Rutt.
"	20		Nothing to report. The front is unusually quiet.	Rutt.
"	21		do.	Rutt.
"	22		do.	Rutt.
"	23		do.	Rutt.
"	24		All quiet.	Rutt.
"	25		A raid was made on the enemy. No prisoners were obtained (Report attached)	Rutt.
"	26		A quiet day.	Rutt.
"	27		ditto. The Battn. was relieved by 1/4th The Duke of Wellington + moved into Divisional Reserve in SIEGE CAMP, VLAMERTINGHE AREA.	Rutt.
SIEGE CAMP	30		Bathing & Interior Economy	Rutt.

A. Dunbar Major
Comdg 1/7th Bn. W. Yorks. Regt.

Confidential

Vol 40

WAR DIARY
of
1/7 Bn. P.W.O. (West Yorkshire Regt.) T.F.
July 1st – 31st. 1918.

Army Form C. 2118.

WAR DIARY
or
INTELLIGENCE SUMMARY.

(Erase heading not required.)

Instructions regarding War Diaries and Intelligence Summaries are contained in F. S. Regs., Part II. and the Staff Manual respectively. Title pages will be prepared in manuscript.

Place	Date	Hour	Summary of Events and Information	Remarks and references to Appendices
	1917			
SIEGE CAMP	1st.		Whole Batn. employed building GREEN LINE through VLAMERTINGHE area	Pratt.
" " "	2nd.		ditto.	Pratt.
" " "	3rd.		ditto.	Pratt.
" " "	4th.		Training.	Pratt.
" " "	5th.		ditto.	Pratt.
" " "	6th.		Training during morning afternoon. Batn. sports gala	Pratt.
" " "	7th.		Church Parade. Batn. moved into Brigade Reserve, S. of YPRES.	Pratt.
Zillebeke	8th.		A quiet day	Pratt.
" "	9th.		ditto.	Pratt.
" "	10th		Nothing to Report	CUA
" "	11		do	CUA
" "	12		do	CUA
" "	13		do	CUA
" "	14		do	CUA
" "	15		Battalion relieved the 16/York R. as Right Battalion of the Right Sector)	CUA

Batn. Mtd. On Front (ZILLEBEKE Sector)

WAR DIARY
or
INTELLIGENCE SUMMARY.
(Erase heading not required.)

Army Form C. 2118.

Instructions regarding War Diaries and Intelligence Summaries are contained in F. S. Regs., Part II. and the Staff Manual respectively. Title pages will be prepared in manuscript.

Place	Date 1918	Hour	Summary of Events and Information	Remarks and references to Appendices
ZILLEBEKE Sect	JULY 16		Nothing to report. - A Coy 117th Infy Regt U.S.A. arrived for attachment for Individual instruction	CWS
do	17		do — 4 platoons of above were attached - 1 to each of our Coys.	CWS
do	18		do — relieved A Coy 1/5 W.Y.R. for 24 hours — One Hq moved to Brandhoek	CWS
do	19		do — A Coy 1/5 W.Y.R. relieved A Coy 117th Infy Regt U.S. - the latter rejoining their own Regt.	CWS
do	20		do — C Coy 117th Infy Regt U.S. Army arrived for attachment for Individual instruction	CWS
do	21		do — the 4 platoons were sent to our Coys — 1 platoon to each by	Batt
do	22		C Coy 117th Infy Regt. (U.S.A.) relieved A Coy 1/7th W.Y.R. - our Coy then moved back to Brown Line	Batt
do	22		The Batt. was relieved in the Line by 1st Batt. 117th Infy Regt. (U.S.R.) Our Batt. then moved to Brown Line	Batt
BROWN LINE	23		The latter was relieved in the Brown Line by 1/6th Duke of Wellington's Regt. Our Batt. then moved to ORILLIA CAMP	Batt
ORILLIA CAMP	24		Rest & further economy bathing.	Batt
do	25		Training - Bathing.	Batt
do	26		do.	Batt
do	27		do.	Army

Army Form C. 2118.

WAR DIARY
or
INTELLIGENCE SUMMARY.
(Erase heading not required.)

Instructions regarding War Diaries and Intelligence Summaries are contained in F.S. Regs., Part II. and the Staff Manual respectively. Title pages will be prepared in manuscript.

Place	Date	Hour	Summary of Events and Information	Remarks and references to Appendices
ORILLIA CAMP	28		Work on GREEN LINE in vicinity of VLAMERTINGHE CHATEAU	Putt.
do	29		do.	Putt.
do	30		The G.O.C. Division presented medal ribbon to the following: Capt. J.W.S. MOORE, M.C. - 2Lieut. N. FEATHER, M.C. - R.Q.M.S. Rhodes M.S.M. - Sgt. Rushing M.S.M. - Sgt. Beevers M.M. - Sgt. Cpl. Metcalfe, M.M. - L/c Strickland, M.M. The G.O.C. also very highly complimented the battn. for the part it played in recent operations - particularly that of the battle of WYTCHAETE RIDGE on 16th April 1918.	
do	31		The battn. moved into the lines on the left of the left Divisional Sector - the extreme left flank of the B.E.F. - relieving the 1/4th ROY.L.I.	Putt. Putt.

R. Dunbar Kruger
Cmdg 1/7th P.W.O (W.York. Rgr.)

Confidential.

War Diary
11th Auxtn. Pl10 (New Zealand Rf. T.F)
1/8/18 — 31/8/18

Vol 41

Army Form C. 2118.

WAR DIARY
or
INTELLIGENCE SUMMARY.

(Erase heading not required.)

1/4th Battn. P.W.O. (West Yorkshire Regt) T.F.

Instructions regarding War Diaries and Intelligence Summaries are contained in F. S. Regs., Part II. and the Staff Manual respectively. Title pages will be prepared in manuscript.

Place	Date 1918	Hour	Summary of Events and Information	Remarks and references to Appendices
YPRES	August.			
	1st.		Battn. in Left Sub-Sector of the Left Brigade. POTIJZE - extreme left flank of B.E.F.	Pl.1
"	2nd.		Nothing to report.	Pl.1/2
"	3rd.		do.	Pl.1/2
"	4th.		do	Pl.1/2
"	5th.		A quiet day.	Pl.1/2
"	6th.		A party of 15 other ranks went to LA LOVIE CHATEAU & were reviewed by the King.	Pl.1/2
"	7th.		A quiet day - nothing to report forward. Transport shelled out of RYDG CAMP moved to BROWNE CAMP.	Pl.1/2
"	8th.		Battn. was relieved by 1/5th. W. Yorks. Regiment & after relief moved into Brigade Reserve N. of YPRES - Battn. H.Q. in YPRES RAMPARTS.	Pl.1/2
"	9th.		Nothing to report.	Pl.1/2
"	10th.		A quiet day.	Pl.1/2
"	11th.		do	Pl.1/2
"	12th.		Nothing to report	Pl.1/2

Army Form C. 2118.

WAR DIARY
or
INTELLIGENCE SUMMARY.
(Erase heading not required.)

1/7th Battn. Prince (West Yorkshire) Regt T.F.

Place	Date 1915	Hour	Summary of Events and Information	Remarks and references to Appendices
YPRES	August 13th		Nothing to Report.	Platt.
"	14th		do	Platt.
"	15th		do	Platt.
"	16th		do	Platt.
BRAKE CAMP 17th			Battn. relieved in Brigade Reserve by 1/7th. Bn. Duke of Wellingtons Regt. On relief Battn. moved to BRAKE CAMP into Divisional Reserve	Platt.
Sheet 28 18th			Rest - bathing - interior economy	CM
PROVEN 19th			Battn. on relief by 1/2th Battn. Suffolk Regt. moved to billets in PROVEN	CM
HERZEELE 20			Battn. marched to HERZEELE	CM
do 21			Training	CM
do 22			do	CM
ZUTKERQUE 23			Battn. moved to ZUTKERQUE (entraining at NORTNERQUE detraining at NORTNERQUE)	CM
LA PANNE 24			Battn. moved to LA PANNE	CM
	25		Training etc. - Lt Col W.R. Pinwill - Kings (Liverpool Regt) assumed Command of Battn.	CM
	26		do	CM
	27		do	CM

Army Form C. 2118.

WAR DIARY
or
INTELLIGENCE SUMMARY.
(Erase heading not required.)

1/7th Anth P.W.O (West Yorkshire Regt) T.F.

Place	Date	Hour	Summary of Events and Information	Remarks and references to Appendices
LA PANNE	28		Battalion moved to TERNAS (LENS 11) via textend train tunnel until entraining at AUDRICQ — Detraining at BRYAS.	CW
TERNAS	29		Interior economy	CW
do	30		Training	CW
do	31		do	CW

C. M. Curnin, Lt. Col.
Commanding 1/7th Battn. P.W.O. (West Yorkshire Regt TF)

9R42

7 West Yorkshire Regiment
War diary
September 1918

Army Form C. 2118.

WAR DIARY
or
INTELLIGENCE SUMMARY.

(Erase heading not required.)

1/7th Battn. W. York Regt.

September 1918

Place	Date	Hour	Summary of Events and Information	Remarks and references to Appendices
TERNAS	1	5.30 pm	Battalion marched to Cross Roads at LA BELLE EPINE & entrained — detraining at LEPENDU	Opps.
Mt. St. ELOY	2		& then marched to OTTAWA CAMP — Mt. St. ELOY area.	Cws
	3		Training	Cws
	4		do	Cws
	5		do	Cws
	6		do	Cws
	7		Brigade Field Exercise	Cws
	8		Church Parade	Cws
	9		Training	Cws
	10		do	Cws
	11		Battn. relieved 7th Battn. Argyle & Sutherland Highlanders at Rly Embankment Camp	Cws
Rly Embankment	12		do do 6th Battn. Gordons & part of the 6½ Batt. Leinsters H.136.9.0 (Sheet 51B.N.W)	Cws
PLOUVAIN	13		Nothing to report	Cws
do	14		do	Cws
do	15		do	Cws
do	16		Battn. on relief by 6th. W. YORK. R. moved to Rly Embankment.	Cws
Rly Embankment	17		Training	Cws
do	18		do	Cws
do	19		do	Cws

Army Form C. 2118.

WAR DIARY
or
INTELLIGENCE SUMMARY.
(Erase heading not required.)

Instructions regarding War Diaries and Intelligence Summaries are contained in F. S. Regs., Part II. and the Staff Manual respectively. Title pages will be prepared in manuscript.

Place	Date	Hour	Summary of Events and Information	Remarks and references to Appendices
Railway Embankment	20		Training. In the evening of this day the Battn. moved up into support in PLOUVAIN Sector - relieving 5th Bn. W.Yorks Rgt.	Auth.
PLOUVAIN Sector	21		Ablutions & Report	Auth. Auth. Auth.
CAM VALLEY	22		ditto	
do	23		Battn. relieved by 7th Black Watch, 6th Black Watch & 7th Gordon Highlanders (51st Div) & moved into Billets in ARRAS	Auth.
ARRAS	24		Interior Economy & Bathing	Auth. Auth. Auth. Auth. Auth. Auth. Auth.
do	25		Training	
do	26		ditto	
do	27		ditto	
do	28		ditto	
do	29		Church Parade & Interior Economy	
do	30		Training	

30/9/18

[signature]
Lt. Col.
Comdg. 7th Bn. W.Yorks Rgt.

1/7th Bn. Pr. O. (West Yorkshire Regt.)

98 A 3

146/49

War Diary
October 1916.

Army Form C. 2118.

WAR DIARY
or
INTELLIGENCE SUMMARY.
(Erase heading not required.)

Place	Date	Hour	Summary of Events and Information	Remarks and references to Appendices
ARRAS	Oct. 1		Training – Batln Platoon Fire Power Contest – Rifles – Revolver & Lewis Gun	Pratt.
do	2		Training	Pratt.
do	3		ditto	Pratt.
do	4		ditto	Pratt.
do	5		ditto	Pratt.
do	6		ditto	Pratt.
do	7		Battn. moved by march & lorries to 51B. V.21.a (CAGNICOURT AREA)	Pratt.
CAGNICOURT	8		Battn. arrived Cagnicourt area at 04.30. After rest – the day was spent in providing reconnaissance.	Pratt.
do	9		Battn. moved by march route to RAILLENCOURT area	Pratt.
RAILLENCOURT	10		The Battn. moved by march route to MORENCHIES (Sheet 51A)	Pratt.
do	11		Battn. moved into assembly position along road between T.12.d 5.6 & 2.9 facing East, preparatory to attack on enemy position on high ground N.W. of AVESNES-L-SEC	Pratt.
IWUY area		04.00	Zero Hour – Barrage opened – the Battn. moved forward to the attack. See official diary attached.	Pratt.
do	12		Captured: About 200 prisoners – 1 field gun – 1 trench mortar battery (4 guns) – many heavy & light machine guns. This attack continued line of railway S.W. of AVESNES-L-SEC captured.	Pratt.
AVESNES-L-SEC area	13		A fairly quiet day.	Pratt.
do	14		Battn. relieved 4th Bn. & 7th Bn. Duke of Wellington Regt. in left sector of R. Subsector of Divisional Front. Battn. H.Q. in VILLERS en CAUCHIES	Pratt.

WAR DIARY
or
INTELLIGENCE SUMMARY.
(Erase heading not required.)

Army Form C. 2118.

Place	Date	Hour	Summary of Events and Information	Remarks and references to Appendices
VILLERS-EN-CAUCHIES	15		Heavy shelling along the whole front	Att.
	16		Battn. relieved 2/4 Bn. Duke of Wellington's Regt. & moved to Sugar Factory U.7.c.1.3. (Sht. 51A)	Att.
	17		Battn. moved by march route to billets in ESCAUDOEUVRES	Att.
ESCAUDOEUVRE	18		Rest + bath.	Att.
	19		Rest + Gulliver economy	Att.
IWUY	20		Battn. moved into billets in IWUY	Att.
do	21		Rest + bath	Att.
do	22		Training	Att.
do	23		do	Att.
do	24		do	Att.
do	25		do	Att.
do	26		do	Att.
do	27		Battn. moved into billets in NOYELLES	Att.
NOYELLES	28		Battn. moved into MAING area in support to 1/5th W.Yorks. Regt. attacking TAMARS	Att.
do	29		Settling & Refit	Att.
do	30		do	
do	31		Battn. moved to TAMARS into assembly positions preparatory to Offensive Action on the morning following.	Att.

J.W. Taylor Lt. Col.
Cmdg 1/7th W.Yorks Regt.

Diary of Action E of CAMBRAI on Oct. 11th 1918.
―oOo―

Reference Map Sheet 51A.

02.30   Battalion in position of assembly along road between
        N.12.d.5.5. and 2.9. facing East.
            Front line Companies :-
                A on the Right.
                B on the Left.
                C in Support.
                D in Reserve.
05.30   Enemy seen taking up positions about 200 yards in front on high
        ground.
07.15. Aerial activity - mostly our own.
07.30. Intermittent shelling of assembly position.
09.00. Zero hour. Barrage opened and the front line Companies went over
        in splendid order. Enemy M.Gs opened heavy fire from ridge in front
09.05. Enemy barrage opened with H.E. gas shell - mostly 5.9 also
        whiz bang.
09.20. Front line Companies over crest of ridge in T.6.d. and U.1.c.
        Prisoners coming in fast - about 500. Many Machine guns captured
        heavy and light.
09.30. Battalion H.Q. moved to top of ridge.
09.43. Lt.Col. W.R. PINWILL D.S.O. Commanding hit by machine gun bullet
        in thigh and carried down.
09.50. Attack still progressing well. C Company report capture of 12
        Field Guns.
10.05. Enemy counter attack launched from railway South of AVESNES le SEC
        accompanied by Tanks. Our troops forced back to crest in U.1.b.
        and 2.a.
10.45   Enemy tanks driven off by concentrated Lewis gun and rifle fire.
10.50. Enemy retiring.
11.00. Front line Battalions (7th and 6th W.Y.R.) reinforced by 5th
        Battalion W.Y.R.and line carried forward to O.32.c. and U.2.b.
        Further advance delayed by disorganization and lack of
        ammunition.   Enemy trench mortar battery captured.
11.30. Further advance impossible owing to casualties. Line in O.32.c.
        and U.2.b. consolidated.
12.00 to 19.00 Heavy enemy shelling and machine gun fire.
20.30. 5th Battalion take over the line 6th and 7th Battns. withdraw to
        reorganize
        Estimated casualties 11 Officers and 400 other ranks.
        The remainder of the day passed with little incident.

Oct. 12th. Advance continued.
            5th W.Y.R. in front line
            6th do. in Support.
            7th do. in Reserve.
09.50. Aircraft report enemy retiring.
10.15. 5th W.Y.R. supported by 6th and 7th Battalions following up in
        retreating enemy.
12.00. 5th W.Y.R. astride railway South of AVESNES-le-SEC and patrols
        out 1000 yards in front.
        The remainder of the day passed without incident
        ―――――

    The following Officers took part in these operations on 11th & 12th
insts.
            A Company. CAPT. J.H.HALL.
                        LT.   S.F.COOK.
                        2/LT. G.H.R.EAKHAM.
                          "   F.J.G.ROBINSON.

B Company.   LT.   GOODALL.
             2/LT.   A.J. IKIN.
              "   J.D. FOSTER.
              "   W.R. JAMES.

C Company.   CAPT.   G.L. HOCKEN.
             2/LT.   W.R. SWARE.
              "   F. BURR.
              "   F. TRIPPS.

D Company.   2/LT.   M. BELL.
              "   C.A. HANCOCK.
              "   M.M. STANFORD.
              "   B.W. MARSHALL.
              "   S.E. LEEDER.

Headquarters. LT. COL. R.W. TINDALL, D.S.O.
              LT.   J. HAYDON.
              2/LT.   F.C. DILLINGER.
              1st LT. L.W. DUPUIS (M.C.O.S.R.)

Confidential.

WAR DIARY
of
1/7th Battn. P.W.O. (West Yorkshire Regt) T.F.

1/11/18 — 30/11/18.

Army Form C. 2118.

WAR DIARY
or
INTELLIGENCE SUMMARY.
(Erase heading not required.)

1/5th Battalion Plato ## West Yorkshire Rgt. T.F.

Instructions regarding War Diaries and Intelligence Summaries are contained in F.S. Regs., Part II. and the Staff Manual respectively. Title pages will be prepared in manuscript.

Place	Date	Hour	Summary of Events and Information	Remarks and references to Appendices
	Nov. 1918			
FAMARS	1		Battn. went into battle in support of 1/5th W. Yorks. Regt. Objective: Railway South of VALENCIENNES. The objective was taken; also large numbers of prisoners, machine guns, trench mortars etc. Casualties very light - a very successful operation. (See Diary of Operations attached)	J.S. 4 4 Auth.
				Auth.
AULNOY	2	02.30	Battn. relieved by 1/4th W. Yorks Inf. Brigade, & moved to railway embankment W. of FAMARS	Auth.
TAMARS	2	16.00	Battn. moved by march route to LIEU ST. AMAND	Auth.
LIEU ST. AMAND	3		Rest & cleaning up. Bathing	Auth.
do	4		Church Parade - Rest - Interior Economy	Auth.
do	5		Battn. moved by march route to EVIN-MALMAISON, N.W. of DOUAI	Auth.
EVIN MALMAISON	6		Cleaning up - rest.	Auth.
do	7		Training & Interior Economy	Auth.
do	8		Training	Auth.
do	9		do	CMS
do	10		Church Parade	CMS
do	11		Armistice signed - Brigade Thanksgiving Service	CMS
do	12 to 30		Training - Educational Scheme in progress	St. Col.

J.S. Foster
Lt. Col.
Commanding 1/5th Bn Plato West Yorkshire Regt. T.F.

War Diary of Operations on November 1st, 1918.

05.00. The Battalion in assembly position in rifle pits W. of FAMARS. Battalion H.Q. in FAMARS. 2nd.Lieut.J.IRWIN killed in action.
Order of Battle;
C.& D.Coys. in Front.
A.& B.Coys. in Support.

05.35. Leading Companies compete 1st.Bound to Rifle Pits E. of FAMARS.

05.45. Zero hour - barrage opens. Heavy shelling by enemy.

06.55. All Companies complete 2nd.Bound across RHONELLE RIVER.

08.20. Battalion H.Q. move forward toward AULNOY. 2nd.Lieut.R.W.McCLURE wounded.

08.45. Companies commence final bound.

09.00. Battalion H.Q. established in AULNOY. Casualties light - many prisoners coming in.

10.00. D.Company sent forward to fill gap in 1/5th.W.Y.R. line.

10.45. Capt. SCHOLFIELD & 2nd.Lieut.BERRY of D.Company wounded. D.Company reach position under heavy shell and machine gun fire.

11.30. C.Company reinforce 1/5th W.Y.R. on the left. Enemy fire still strong.

12.15. Situation on right obscure. Right flank of the 1/5th. W.Y.R. in the air. A.Company sent to form defensive flank on Right.

14.00. Right flank secured.

15.00. Situation quiet.
16.00. Enemy aircraft active.

16.30. Enemy shelling heavily. Enemy counter attack develops.

17.30. Counter attack repulsed - mainly the result of exellent work by A.Company, *as concerning our front.*

18.00. Situation quiet.

19.00.to 23.99. A very dark night. Situation quiet.

November 2nd.

02.30. The Battalion relieved by 148th.Infantry Brigade, moves back to Railway Embankment W. of FAMARS.

Casualties.
5 Officers
56 Other Ranks.

The following Officers took part in this operation.

A. Company.

Lieut. E.A. SWIFT.
2nd. Lieut. C.B. MORTIMER.

B. Company.

Capt. W.J.S. MOORE, M.C.
2nd. Lieut. J. JEWITT

C. Company.

Lieut. C.J.B SMITH
2nd. Lieut. F.W. TENNANT
H. ALLAN

D. Company.

Capt. W.S. SCHOLFIELD
2nd. Lieut. H. BERRY
2nd. Lieut. R.R. WHITTAKER

Battn. H.Q.

Lieut. Colonel J.A. FOXTON
Capt. J. RHODES
Lieut. P.M. HAYDON.
2/Lieut. R.V. McCLURE

Copy of message received from Corps Commander, XXII Corps.

2nd. November, 1918.

G.O.C. 49th. Division.

I wish to heartily congratulate you and your Division on the successful capture of all your objectives and the heavy losses inflicted on the enemy as the result of your two days hard and gallant fighting.

All three Infantry Brigades, your Artillery and Engineers, have added another page to the distinguished record of the Division.

From GENERAL GODLEY, XXII Corps.

146th. Infantry Brigade.

I send you herewith a copy of a message from the Corps Commander XXII. Corps.

My own very hearty congratulations go with it.

Apart from the actual fighting, you have all had many serious difficulties, and much hard work to contend with, especially in connection with the rapid changes in plan brought about by frequent changes in the situation.

I admire immensely the spirit of initiative and enthusiasm with which Infantry, Artillery and Engineers alike have met and overcome those difficulties, and much hard and I congratulate you all most warmly on the well earned success which has crowned your efforts.

You have, indeed, added an honourable page to the history of the 49th.(West Riding) DIVISION.

(sd) N.G.CAMERON. Major-General,
3rd. November, 1918   Commanding 49th.(West Riding) Division.

1/5th.Bn.W.York.R.
1/6th. -do-
1/7th. -do-
146th.Trench Mortar Battery.

Forwarded.

(sd) F.H.WITTS, Captain,
3/11/18   Brigade Major, 146th.Infantry Brigade.

Confidential

98 + 5

WAR DIARY

of

1/4th Bn. P.W.O. (West Yorkshire Regt.) T.F.

December 1st. 1918
to
31st. 1918.

Army Form C. 2118.

WAR DIARY
or
INTELLIGENCE SUMMARY.

(Erase heading not required.) 1/17th Bn. P.W.O. (West Yorkshire Regt) T.F.

Place	Date	Hour	Summary of Events and Information	Remarks and references to Appendices
EVIN-MALMAISON	1918 DECEMBER			
	1st		Church Parade.	Nil
	2nd to 7th		Salvage, Interior Economy, Parade etc.	Nil
	8th		Church Parade.	Nil
	9th to 14th		Parade, Salvage, etc.	Nil
	15th		Church Parade	Nil
	16th		Inspection of the Division by Lieut. General Sir A.J. GODLEY, K.C.B., K.C.M.G., Comdg. XIII Corps. (See Special Order of the day attached.)	Nil
	17th to 21st		Parade, Salvage, etc.	Nil
	22nd		Church Parade	Nil
	23rd		Salving (Parades)	Nil
	24th		Christmas day. – Church Parade – Mens Christmas Dinner – Concert etc.	Nil
	25th		Boxing day. – Amusement etc.	Nil
	26th		Salvage.	Nil
	27th		Cleaning out of Billets.	Nil
	28th		Church Parade	Nil
	29th		Salvage.	Nil
	30th		Parade	Nil
	31st			Nil

J.A. Forto
Lt. Col.
Comdg 1/17th W.Yorks. Regt.

Enclosure to

Special ORDER OF THE DAY.

by

Major General N.J.G. Cameron, C.B., C.M.G.,

Commanding 49th (West Riding) Division.

From:- Lieutenant General Alex. J. Godley, K.C.B., K.C.M.G.,
Commanding XXII Corps:-

To:- Major General N.J.G. Cameron, C.B., C.M.G.,
Commanding 49th (West Riding) Division.

16th December, 1918.

I must write to tell you how much I appreciated your kind thought in asking me to inspect your Division to-day and giving me the chance of seeing all together the 49th (W.R.) Division, which is so closely identified with this Corps and which I have had the good fortune to have under my command in so many hard fights. At Passchendaele last Autumn, all through the winter in the Ypres salient, on the Vierstraat line in the Spring of this year and latterly about Arras and from Cambrai to Valenciennes in the concluding stages of the war, your Division has fought in this Corps and has always proved itself one of the best and stoutest Divisions that we have ever had. I think you all know my feelings towards the Division and how glad I have always been to have it with me and this feeling is shared by the whole of the Corps Staff. To-day I was proud and felt it a great honour to receive the salute of such men as yours and I would ask you to convey to all ranks my heartiest congratulations on their appearance and turn-out. Nothing could have been better. Their steadiness and discipline were evident and their drill and march-past first rate; That the Artillery should have been able to trot past so well in such deep ground speaks volumes for their training. Wishing you and the Division the best of luck in the future and with again my warmest thanks and congratulations.

Believe me
Yours very sincerely,
(sd) Alex: J. Godley.

From:- Major General N.J.G. Cameron, C.B., C.M.G.,
Commanding 49th (West Riding) Division.

To:- Lieutenant General A.J. Godley, K.C.B., K.C.M.G.,
Commanding XXII Corps.

18th December, 1918.

Thank you very warmly for your kind letter - and once more thank you very much for coming all the way from Mons to inspect the Division on the 16th. I had felt sure you would come if you could and I had ventured to believe that having come, you would enjoy seeing the whole Division on parade.

Believe me, General, the 49th (West Riding) Division is mindful and proud of the fact that it has often served in the XXII Corps under your command in stirring times.

We much appreciated your coming on the 16th and I know that all ranks will much appreciate your kind words when I send them out as I am doing now.

With the heartiest of good wishes for Christmastide and the New Year from the 49th (West Riding) Division to yourself and the XXII Corps.

Yours very sincerely,
(sd) Neville G. Cameron.

SPECIAL ORDER OF THE DAY

by

Major General N.J.G.Cameron, C.B,C.M.G.,

Commanding 49th (West Riding) Division.

18th December, 1918.

Officers, Non-commissioned Officers, and men, of the 49th

(West Riding) Division,

Enclosed you will find the copy of a letter which I have been proud to receive to-day from Lieutenant General Sir A.Godley K.C.B., K.C.M.G., Commanding the XXII Corps, who inspected the Division on Monday 16th December, and under whose command the Division has been so often, during fighting operations. I trust and believe that it will be as pleasant reading to you as it was to me.

Enclosed you will also find a copy of my reply, to show you that in your name I have thanked Lieutenant General Sir A.Godley for his very real interest in the Division.

There can be no question but that on 16th December every unit in the Division distinguished itself by its turnout and by the admirable manner in which it marched past.

Artillery, Engineers, Infantry, Light Trench Mortar Batteries, Machine Gunners, Field Ambulances, Train, Mechanical Transport Coy. and Mobile Veterinary Section, one and all showed by the smart and soldierly turn-out of their personnel and their transport, and by their good drill, that they had thoroughly realised that whatever has to be done is worth doing well, - a spirit which I am proud and happy to think has actuated the 49th (West Riding) Division in all its fighting operations.

Well done !

(signed) N.G.Cameron, Major General,
Commanding 49th (West Riding) Division.

NOTE. - The General has informed us that the march past of this
Battalion was the best in the Division.

Confidential.

WAR DIARY
of
1/7th Battn. P.W.O. (West Yorkshire Regt T.F.)

1/1/19 — 31/1/19.

98 46

Army Form C. 2118.

WAR DIARY
or
INTELLIGENCE SUMMARY. 1/7th Battn. W. York. Regt.

(Erase heading not required.)

Instructions regarding War Diaries and Intelligence Summaries are contained in F. S. Regs., Part II. and the Staff Manual respectively. Title pages will be prepared in manuscript.

Place	Date 1919 JANUARY	Hour	Summary of Events and Information	Remarks and references to Appendices
EVIN MALMAISON	1 to 4		Training, Salvaging, etc. Recreational games	cus.
do	5		Church Parade	cus
do	6-11		Training, Salvaging, etc. Recreational games	cus
do	12		Church Parade	cus
do	13-14		Training, Salvaging etc. Recreational games	cus.
do	15		Battalion marched to LOOS - 1 mile S.W. of LILLE	cus
do	16		Battalion spent the day in LILLE, dinner at E.F.C. and attended the Theatre	cus.
LOOS	17		Battalion marched back to hutts at EVIN MALMAISON	cus
EVIN MALMAISON	18			cus
do	19		Church Parade	
do	20-25		Training, Salvage, etc. Recreational games	cus
do	26		Church Parade	cus
do	27-31		Training, Salvage, etc. Recreational games	cus

J.W. Forster
Lt. Col.
Commanding 1/7th Battn. West Yorkshire Regt. T.F.

Army Form C. 2118.

WAR DIARY
or
INTELLIGENCE SUMMARY. 1/7th Battalion P.W.O. West York Regt T.F.
(Erase heading not required)

N4L 4 7

Place	Date	Hour	Summary of Events and Information	Remarks and references to Appendices
ENIN MALMAISON	Feby 1		Training etc - Games.	APP
	2		Church Parade	APP
	3-8		Training Salvaging etc - Games	APP
	9		Church Parade	APP
	10-15		Training Salvaging etc - Games	APP
	16		Church Parade	APP
	17-22		Training, Salvaging etc - Games	APP
	23		Church Parade -	APP
			One Officer and 100 O.Rs posted to 1/6 Bt West Yorkshire Regt which proceeded to the Army of Occupation the next day	APP
	24-28		Training Salvaging etc - Games	APP
	28		22 O.Rs posted to 1/5th Bt West Yorkshire Reg t to proceed to Army of Occupation -	APP
			A very large number of men were demobilized during the month -	APP

Dunbar Thya
Cdg 1/7 Bt W. York Regt

CONFIDENTIAL

WAR DIARY
OF
1/7 Batt. P.W.O (West Yorkshire Regiment)
1-3-19 — 31-3-19

WV 48

WAR DIARY
INTELLIGENCE SUMMARY. 1/7th Bn. PWO (WEST YORKSHIRE RGT)

Army Form C. 2118.

MARCH - 1919

Place	Date 1919 March	Hour	Summary of Events and Information	Remarks and references to Appendices
EVIN MALMAISON	1		Training = 9 Officers and 196 O.R. posted to 1/5th Battn. W. York Rgt.	CMS
do	2		do	CMS
do	3		Moved to DOUAI	CMS
DOUAI	4 to 31.		During this time the battalion was gradually reduced to Cadre strength - which it reached the last day of the month -	CMS

8.4.19

Dunbar Dryan
Cdg 1/7 & 8th West Yorkshire Regt.

98 49

Confidential

War Diary
of
17th Bn. West Yorkshire Regt.

1/4/19 — 30/4/19.

WAR DIARY
or
INTELLIGENCE SUMMARY. 1/7th W.York. Regiment.

Army Form C. 2118.

APRIL 1919

Place	Date 1919	Hour	Summary of Events and Information	Remarks and references to Appendices
DOUAI	April 1st to 30th.		Salvage	C.W.R.

A. Dunbar Major
Commanding 1/7 W.York Rgt.

98150

Confidential

War Diary
of
1/4th Battn. P.W.O. (West Yorkshire Regt. T.F.)

1/5/19 — 31/5/19

MAY 1919

Army Form C. 2118.

WAR DIARY
or
INTELLIGENCE SUMMARY.
(Erase heading not required.)

1/2nd Bn. W.York Rgt.

Place	Date	Hour	Summary of Events and Information	Remarks and references to Appendices
DOUAI	May 1st to 31		Battalion returned to Crewe — Nothing of interest to report	EM

C.M. Sewell Capt
Comndg 1/7 W.York Rgt